Teaching Art in Primary Schools

Teaching ART
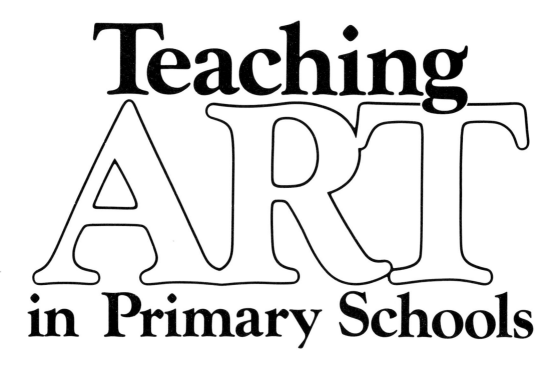

in Primary Schools

A development through activities

Geoff Rowswell

CollinsEducational
An imprint of HarperCollinsPublishers

Published by
CollinsEducational
An imprint of HarperCollins*Publishers*
77–85 Fulham Palace Road
Hammersmith
London W6 8JB

First published in 1983 by
Evans Brothers Ltd

Reprinted 1985, 1987, 1989, 1991

ISBN 0–00–312524–6

Printed in Great Britain at
The Bath Press, Avon

Contents

Acknowledgements

I am indebted to the children who have provided this book with so many visually exciting examples, and to their teachers who have kindly allowed me to photograph their work. My gratitude goes particularly to those teachers who offered practical help and guidance in the planning of sessions; Lorna Archer, Sue Baker, Sue Budd, Anita Creese, Enid Howard, Jennie Morris, Paul Murphy, Sue Scott, Rosemary Smith, Sue Smith, Peter White and Christine Wyard; and to Mr Collins of Cherry Orchard Primary School, Worcester and Mr J. Morris of Malvern Wells C.E. Primary School who allowed me to photograph children at work in their schools.

A special thank you to my wife, Mary, who has provided constant support and also acted as proof reader and typist, and to my four girls for their invaluable clerical assistance.

To American readers

Where the term primary is used, this refers to the age range five to eleven years. Most children in the United Kingdom do not start school before the age of five. There are different types of schools serving the primary range.

1. 5– 7 years   Infant school } These are usually situated close to each
2. 7–11 years   Junior school } other.
3. 5–11 years   Primary school.
4. 5– 9 years   First school.

Children will transfer from the infant school to the junior school.
Children will transfer from the junior and primary schools directly to secondary school (equivalent to a high school).
Children will transfer from the first school to middle school, (equivalent to a junior high school).

To Teachers and Student Teachers

The aim of this book is to provide the non art-specialist teacher with the framework of a co-ordinated scheme for teaching the basic concepts of art to primary school children, which will form a basis for art education at a later stage.

The Sessions outlined in this book aim to provide a continuous sequence of experiences that slowly build up artistic concepts and skills. The number of Sessions at each stage is regarded as the *minimum* necessary for an adequate scheme, and it is hoped that teachers will enlarge and develop the scheme by including other lessons to suit individual requirements.

The scheme is in six stages. The ages given are intended only as a rough guide, as much depends on previous experience.

Stage 1	5– 6 years	30 sessions
Stage 2	6– 7 years	30 sessions
Stage 3	7– 8 years	15 sessions
Stage 4	8– 9 years	15 sessions
Stage 5	9–10 years	15 sessions
Stage 6	10–11 years	15 sessions

The length of a Session can vary tremendously, and is not necessarily designed as a single lesson. Once again, much depends on the interest of the children and the method of working on the part of the teacher. All Sessions outlined in the book have been tried and tested by experienced primary teachers who are *not* art specialists.

The illustrations are not meant to indicate the most desired results to be expected, but should help readers to predict and visualise likely results from children at a particular stage of development. It is hoped that this will prove helpful to teachers and parents with little experience of teaching primary children, and who find it difficult to anticipate the capabilities of young children.

Organisation

Methods of teaching art in primary schools vary tremendously and I am not recommending one method in preference to another. So much depends on the constraints of the classroom. In some cases art might be a whole class activity and in others, especially where space is limited, teachers prefer to organise small group activities. Some children will be doing art and others will, perhaps, be doing writing, which doesn't require so much space. In many infant classes art is one of the creative activities that children work at alongside water and sand play, doing jigsaws, etc.

No definite time limit is envisaged for the following Sessions, therefore, and it is left to the discretion of individual teachers how each Session should be organised. Teachers would do well to remember, however, that plenty of time should be allowed for children to *complete* creative work. It is no good stopping a child when he is successfully engrossed in a piece of art work and expecting him to continue with it the following week, when the inspiration and inclination has usually gone. Young children are very much creatures of the moment; so if a child is engaged in making a model when the bell goes for the end of the lesson or day, he should be allowed time at the beginning of the next lesson or day to complete his work while the impetus is still there. This calls for a flexible approach on the part of the teacher, but the results from children should be well worth minor inconveniences.

As in the case of teaching any subject, the key to good art teaching lies largely in the teacher's ability to prepare a lesson and then to present it to the children. In the case of art this usually involves making a list of the materials needed, how the room is to be arranged and what form the introduction will take. The teacher must try to anticipate how the lesson will progress and plan accordingly. The corrolation between a teacher's ability to do these things, and her own artistic ability, is not necessarily high. In fact some of the most successful primary art teaching is carried out by teachers who make no claims to being artistic themselves.

Each Session outlined in this book is designed with these points in mind, but the success of each depends largely on:
a) The teacher's confidence with the materials – so new techniques should be tried out first to learn the pitfalls.
b) The quality of the stimulus materials – whether pictures are appropriate, tatty, large enough to see at the back, etc.
c) The enthusiasm shown by the teacher – the most important point.
Teaching art properly can be extremely demanding, both physically and mentally. The rewards, in terms of personal satisfaction, pleasure for the children and educational benefits in other subject areas, are generally well worth the effort.

Stages 1 and 2 – infants

Each stage comprises thirty Sessions, allowing for about ten Sessions each term. However, these two stages have been designed to allow for a certain amount of overlapping, as many Infant classes have children of five, six and seven years in them, and teachers may prefer to teach stages 1 and 2 simultaneously.

Each Session aims either to introduce or increase awareness of an artistic concept or concepts, which are stated at the beginning of each Session outline. It is hoped that teachers will augment these Sessions with others that will further increase awareness of these concepts, and also allow the children time to develop newly-acquired skills.

Most activities will tend to be of an exploratory nature, and emphasis should be placed on what experiences children are gaining, rather than on what the finished product looks like.

Children should be urged to study things, not just by looking, but touching (with eyes closed), smelling and tasting (when safe to do so). Microscopes and magnifying glasses are useful aids.

Objective work should be balanced with opportunities for children to indulge their fantasies. The aim should be to direct children away from the usual stereotypes that they acquire from comics and television.

Stage 1

Stage 2

Activity:	Scribbling and doodling.
Concept:	Line/mark-making.
Aim:	To introduce the children to a range of mark-making tools.

Resources needed:	*All groups:* Newspaper; any cheap paper, preferably white. *Group A:* Wax crayons; pencils; felt-tip pens; ball-point pens; charcoal; chalk. *Group B:* Twigs; matchsticks; feathers; strips of card, etc.; runny paint in paste jars, one per child. *Group C:* Same as for Group B but instead of paint, improvise with home-made 'paint' made from runny mud, cocoa, etc.
Preparation:	Cut paper into pieces approximately 20 × 30 cm. Cover tables with newspaper. Children to mix up their own 'paint' beforehand.
Introduction:	Explain that they are not necessarily expected to draw pictures, but simply to try out all the different materials. Offer suggestions by demonstrating some of them, then allow exploration by themselves.
Development:	Children could start off in groups but they may move from table to table, taking their paper with them. Plenty of praise and encouragement for any results produced will spur on the children to experimentation. Some will naturally draw representational images, usually Mum, others will be content with random marks that represent absolutely nothing. There will be a tendency to expect recognisable images and to especially praise those that appear, but this should be resisted. Each child's efforts should be received equally, with nothing but praise and admiration. When applicable, introduce words that describe particular qualities of line: wiggly, jumpy, dotty, etc.
Evaluation:	Did the children seem to enjoy themselves? Were they keen to try out different tools? Could they express with words some of the lines that they had made?

Activity: Experiments with lines.

Concept: Line.

Aim: To develop skill in handling materials.
To make children aware that there are many ways of making lines.

Resources needed: The same as for Session 1.

Preparation: The same as for Session 1. Display the results of Session 1. Try to ensure that each child has something displayed.

Introduction: Discuss some of the results of Session 1, paying attention to the different sorts of lines. Give the lines adjectives that describe the quality of each: jagged, jerky, wiggly, etc. Find nice things to say about the work: I like this long, wiggly red line; don't you? Encourage similar comments from the children about one anothers' work.

Development: Children could start off in the same groups as for Session 1 and move round when you feel they are ready. Paper is placed vertically and the children are asked to make lines going horizontally across their paper. They should try out each tool in turn and aim to make lines which have different qualities. Keep reminding them of the words already used and praise children who invent new lines or words. Some lines will flow gracefully, others will be broken and hesitant, changing in character as the paint runs out or blobs. Encourage them to pack as many lines as possible on to their paper, which will probably resemble interference on a television screen. If there is time at the end of the Session, ask some of the children to talk about their lines.

Evaluation: Did the children seem to enjoy themselves?
Were they more confident than during Session 1?
Could they remember any of the words used?
Could they describe their own lines?

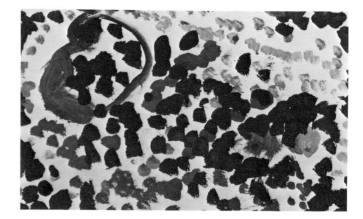

Activity: Exploring paint.

Concept: Colour.

Aim: To introduce the children to painting materials.

Resources needed: Newspapers; any cheap paper; water jars, one between two; paint rags, one each; several pots of thick creamy paint for each group; one large paint brush each.

Preparation: Cut paper into pieces approximately 40 × 30 cm. Cover tables with newspaper and mix the paints. Give out materials. Prepare a place where the paintings will dry without overlapping such as a string washing line with paper clips or pegs to hang them.

Introduction: Ask the children to have the colours in front of them. Demonstrate to the children how to use the paints without mixing the colours in the jar. Take a brushful of one colour and make some dots on the paper, wash the brush then dry it on a paint rag. Dip it into a second colour and paint some more dots.

Development: Ask the children to do a painting of dots that go all over the paper. Use all the available colours, but try not to mix them in the jar. Always make sure that the brush is clean before putting it into the new colour.
When the children have finished their painting of dots, ask them to do a second painting. This time they may use the paint in any way they like on the paper; but the paint in the jars must remain clean as before. Encourage spreading one colour across another so that they mix. Recognisable objects are not essential but may well appear. The accent should be on enjoying using thick paint, rather than making pictures.
Allow time to discuss the paintings (not pictures). Ask the children to describe the colours that they have used, and whether any new colours were made by accident.

Evaluation: Did the children enjoy this Session?
Were they able to describe their paintings?

Activity: Learning to use paint.

Concept: Colour/line.

Aim: To introduce the children to different-sized brushes.
To introduce the primary colours.

Resources needed: Newspaper; any cheap, white paper; water jars, one between two; one paint rag each; yellow, red and blue paint; one large and one small brush each; jars for paint, three to a group.

Preparation: Cut the paper into pieces approximately 40 × 30 cm. Cover tables with newspaper. One-third fill jars with thick, creamy paint. The consistency is important, see notes on paints on page 155. Give out a jar of blue, red and yellow to each group. Give out other materials.

Introduction: Ask the children the names of the colours in front of them. Red, yellow, blue; known as the primary colours. Remind the children how they drew different sorts of lines across the paper in Session 2. Today lines will be made with paint and brushes. Remind them of some of the types of line that they made: wiggly, jerky, rough, etc. Demonstrate different ways of using the brush: dragging lightly, pushing heavily, stippling, etc. Demonstrate how to wash and dry the brush before changing colour.

Development: Tell the children to dip one of their brushes in one of the colours and make a line that goes right across the paper in a line. Use the same colour to make two more, but different types of line. Wash and dry the brush, then do three lines with the second colour. Wash and dry the brush, then do three lines with the third. Change brushes and repeat the process until the paper is filled with lines. If there is time, let them paint lines that go all over the paper. Remember to praise every effort. Questions should consolidate knowledge of the primaries: Which colour have you used most? Which one the least?, etc.

Evaluation: Did the children enjoy this?
Did the children remember much about lines?
Did they learn what the primaries are?

Activity: Learning about red.

Concept: Colour/tone.

Aim: To make the children aware of the different reds that exist in their environment.
To demonstrate that a colour can vary in *tone*.

Resources needed: As many different red backing materials as you can find: paper, Cellophane, tissue paper, etc. A selection of red objects. Reproductions of paintings or magazine photographs where red is the predominant colour.

Preparation: Cut the many different plain red paper or material to the same size – about 15 × 20 cm. Prepare a table with display board behind, preferably in the classroom. Cover the surfaces with red paper or material, ready for the children's offerings. Tell the children to bring in things from home that are *entirely* red, and to put them on the table.

Introduction: Ask the children to talk about the things brought from home and ask questions aimed at increasing their understanding of red. What colour is it? Can you see something else on the display or in the room that is the same *shade* of red as your object? Put it alongside to make sure. Is John's red car lighter or darker than Susan's red skirt? Can you see two things that are the same red exactly?

Development: Children to rearrange the things on display so that the objects are in groups of the same shade of red. Put the lightest reds on one end of the table and the darkest on the opposite end. Do the same with the red papers so that you have a *tonal scale* going from light to dark. Children could work individually or in groups.
Try to think of names for all the different reds so that you can identify them, e.g. tomato, pillar box, blood, etc. Label objects on display.

Evaluation: Did the display generate interest?
Did the introduction spark off plenty of discussion?
Were the children able to make a tonal scale of reds?

Activity:	Painting tints and shades of red.	
Concept:	Colour.	
Aim:	To increase awareness of the colour red. To teach how to make tints and shades of a colour.	

Resources needed: Newspaper; any cheap, white paper; water jars, one between two; paint rags, one each; red, white and black paints; large brushes; jars for paint, three to a group; mixing palettes, one each. If possible, have more than one red, e.g. crimson and vermilion.

Preparation: Cut paper into pieces approximately 40 × 30 cm.
Cover tables with newspaper.
One-third fill jars with paint of a thick creamy consistency. The consistency is important. See notes on mixing on page 155.
Give out brushes, rags, jars, palettes and paper.

Introduction: Demonstrate how to make a tint by putting some red paint into the palette and adding a little white. Demonstrate how to make a shade by putting some red into the palette and adding a tiny bit of black. The brush must always be washed and dried before dipping it into a different colour.

Development: Remind children of the different reds on their display and invite them to fill their paper with as many reds as they like. Allow time for discussion about the results.

Evaluation: Was this Session enjoyable?
Were the children able to discuss their results?
Could they say how they made tints and shades?

Activity: Painting a red dragon.

Concept: Colour.

Aim: To increase awareness of the colour red.
To consolidate the introduction to tints and shades.

Resources needed:
1. Newspapers; any cheap, white paper; water jars, one between two; paint rags, one each; red, white and black paints – if possible have a deep crimson or scarlet; mixing palettes, one each; large brushes; paint jars.
2. Stories or poems about dragons, e.g. 'The Dragon' from the Faerie Queen.

Preparation: Display results of the previous session.
Cut the paper into strips approximately 20 × 5 cm.
Cover tables with newspapers.
One-third fill jars with thick creamy paint.
Give out painting materials.

Introduction: Read the stories or poems about dragons. Tell your own story about a long, wiggly dragon who had a stripy pattern all over him in many shades of red.

Development: Remind the children how they made tints and shades in the previous session.
Give out the strips of paper and ask the children to mix one tint or shade of red in their palette and then to paint their strip with it. Try to get it as even as possible. Tell them to put this strip on one side to dry. They then add more red or white to their palette or tiny amounts of black to make further tints or shades, which they use to paint other strips. Remind them how to keep the colours in the jars clean by washing and drying their brushes each time. When the strips are dry the children should place them in a tonal scale on the floor – the darkest strip at one end and the lightest at the opposite. This should cause a lot of discussion. Finally, the teacher might display these strips on the wall with a dragon's head that either she or one of the children has made.

Evaluation: Did the children remember how to make tints and shades?
Were they better at handling the paint this session?

Activity: Painting flames.

Concept: Colour.

Aim: To encourage children to be aware of the colours of flames. To provide the opportunity to mix flame colours.

Resources needed: Newspaper; any cheap paper; water jars, one between two; primary colours plus black and white; brushes; jars for paint, full range for each group; mixing palettes, one each; candle; matches; large bowl of water.

Preparation: Cut paper to about three different sizes.
Cover the tables with newspaper.
One-third fill jars with thick, creamy paint.
Give out other materials.
Display the dragon produced in Session 7.
Make a taper by tightly rolling half a sheet of paper.

Introduction: Discuss the dragon and ask if anything is missing. Flames from his mouth! Ask what colours appear in flames. Light a candle and ask the same question. Blow it out. Light the taper and discuss the different colours. Extinguish it by dropping it into the bowl of water.
Invite the children to paint some flames for the dragon's mouth, and then perhaps a candle flame, or their fire at home.

Development: Remind the children how to keep the colours in the jars clean by washing and drying brushes each time. Remind them how to lighten colours and encourage them to mix the primary colours in order to get other colours that they need. It is better that they should discover for themselves what happens when red and yellow are mixed, rather than be told how to make orange.

Evaluation: Did the children's paintings suggest flames?
Did they handle the paint properly?

Activity: Bonfire paintings.

Concept: Colour.

Aim: To encourage children to express an idea through paint. To consolidate previous work on colour.

See Colour Plate N

Resources needed: Newspaper; any cheap paper; water jars, one between two; paint rags, one each; primary colours, plus black and white; brushes; jars for paint; mixing palettes, one each.

Preparation: Cut paper to approximately 40 × 30 cm.
Cover tables with newspaper.
One-third fill jars with thick, creamy paint.
Give out other materials.
Display paintings from Session 8.

Introduction: Refer to the paintings on display and ask children to describe a bonfire party that they attended. Remind children about keeping paints in the jars clean, then invite them to paint the bonfire and some of the fireworks that they saw.

Development: Time should be allowed to discuss the results. Encourage children to say how colours were mixed, how many tints or shades of the same colour appear, how many different colours appear, etc.

Evaluation: Did the paintings suggest the excitement of a bonfire party?
Were the children able to mix appropriate colours and remember what was meant by tint and shade?

Activity: Paper sculpture – Nativity scene.

Concept: Pattern/shape.

Aim: To introduce simple paper sculpture techniques.
To make children aware of the shapes and patterns in snowflakes and how to express some of them.

Resources needed:
1. Thin white card; thin white paper; felt-tip pens; scissors; pencils.
2. Story and pictures of the Nativity.
3. Enlarged pictures of snowflakes.

Preparation: Cut the card to approximately 20 × 15 cm.
Cut the paper to approximately 10 × 10 cm.

Introduction: Read the story of the Nativity and show the pictures. Discuss the clothes being worn in the picture and ask if any pattern can be seen on the clothes. What is it like? Show the pictures of snowflakes and discuss the patterns. Tell the children that they will be drawing and cutting out the Nativity scene, and also making snowflakes for the background.
Volunteers are needed to make the central characters. The other children can choose to make angels, shepherds and snowflakes.

Development: *Group A:* Figures and angels. Make a crease lengthways down the centre of the card. Flatten the card and draw the outline of the figure in pencil so that the crease runs through middle. Add details and patterns with felt-tip pen, then cut away the background. Ensure that the base of the figure is flat, so that it will stand when the card is creased slightly.
Group B: Snowflakes. Use any circular objects as templates to draw circles on the paper. Cut out the circles. Fold the circle in half, then in half again. Cut small shapes from the straight creases and the circular edge to make snowflake patterns.

Evaluation: Did they enjoy this session?
Did the results indicate that some thought had been given to patterning the clothes, and how to cut the snowflake patterns?

Activity:	Taking a line for a walk on graph paper.
Concept:	Line.
Aim:	To develop skill in hand to eye movement.

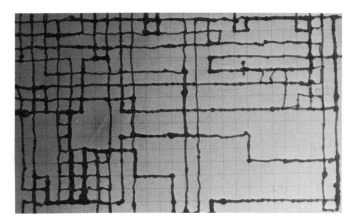

Resources needed:	Pencils; felt-tip pens; ball-point pens; graph paper with 1 cm squares.
Preparation:	Cut graph paper to approximately 20 × 30 cm. Ask children to choose one drawing instrument.
Introduction:	Explain that they are going to take a line for a walk over graph paper, but that it must stay on the graph lines. Starting on any of the graph lines, move the line along slowly. It may change direction as often as it likes and can cross over itself, but the pen or pencil must not be lifted from the paper until the line has wandered all over the paper and then returned to its original starting point. Demonstrate this.
Development:	Tell the children not to worry if the line wobbles off or slips off the graph line. The important thing is to show it *all* of the paper, moving slowly and thinking carefully about where they are going. If the children rush back to the starting point without fully exploring the paper, make another starting point. Allow time to discuss the different arrangements of lines. At which part of the paper did the pencil spend most time? How do you know? Which are the longest lines? Who has made the longest line of all? Can you see where the line started and finished?
Evaluation:	Did the children enjoy this session? Was there much discussion about the finished results?

Activity: Taking a line for a walk on plain paper.

Concept: Line/shape.

Aim: To develop skill in handling drawing instruments.
To make children aware that lines enclose shapes.

Resources needed: Crayons; pencils; felt-tip pens; ball-point pens; any cheap, light-coloured paper.

Preparation: Cut the paper to about 20 × 30 cm.
Ask the children to choose a drawing implement that they did not use for Session 11.
Display the results of Session 11. Try to ensure that each child has something displayed.

Introduction: Remind the children of Session 11, and discuss some of the results. Explain that they are going to take another line for a walk, but this time there are no graph lines to keep to. They must start and finish at the same place, and walk their line all over their paper, but this time they don't have to go in a straight line. They can invent their own paths, which might be wavy, zig-zag, curly or bumpy, but once the line is started the pen or pencil must not lift off the paper until it has returned to its starting point. Lines may cross over one another or completely avoid one another.

Development: Tell the children not to rush and to think where their line is going and what sort of path it is taking. When they have finished, ask them to put a dot on any enclosed shapes that the line has made. The tiny shapes could be filled in with pen or pencil, and the large ones with crayon. Allow time to discuss the finished results. Which designs haven't got any enclosed shapes? Why is this? Which have got lots? Why? What sort of shapes are there? Are any shapes repeated?

Evaluation: Did the children enjoy this session?
Was there much discussion about the finished results?
Were many different types of lines invented?

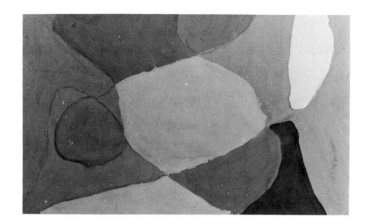

Activity: Painting shapes.

Concept: Colour.

Aim: To consolidate children's understanding of the primary colours.

See Colour Plate K

Resources needed: Newspaper; any cheap white paper; water jars, one between two; paint rags, one each; red, blue and yellow paint for each group; two brushes for each child, one size 4 and one size 12.

Preparation: Cut paper into pieces approximately 40 × 30 cm.
Cover tables with newspaper.
Children to mix and fill the jars to one-third with paint of a creamy consistency. The consistency is very important. Children will not get the same sensuous delight from using colour if the paint is watery or has to be scrubbed from a block. If children are taught to mix paints at this stage, there will be less waste later on and more time for the teacher. See notes on mixing, page 155.
Give out brushes, rags, paper and water jars.
Prepare a place where paintings will dry without overlapping or string up a washing line to hang them with paper clips or pegs.

Introduction: Ask the children to name the three colours that are in front of them. Red, yellow, blue. Ask what another name for them is? Primary colours.

Development: Remind children of the time they took lines for a walk (Session 12). Dip the smaller of their two brushes in any one of the colours and take that colour line for a walk, so that they make little and big enclosed shapes. Fill in the little shapes with the little brush, and the big shapes with the big brush. Always wash and dry the brush before dipping it into a different colour. Fill every bit of the paper with colour. If there is time to do another painting they could paint a happy picture with these happy colours.
The teacher should praise every child's results. Questions should consolidate knowledge of the primaries. Who has a lot of red in their painting? Who has more blue than yellow? Did anyone mix the colours accidentally? What new colour did you get? Who would like to tell us about their happy picture?

Evaluation: Was this Session enjoyable?
Did the children follow your instructions?
Were the results what you expected?

Activity: Painting textures.

Concept: Texture.

Aim: To encourage the children to express texture through the medium of paint.

Resources needed:
1. Newspapers; any cheap, white paper; water jars, one between two; paint rags, one each; red, blue and yellow paint for each group; brushes; overalls.
2. Small quantities of sand, sawdust, etc. for each group.
3. Any natural objects that have a rough surface: bark, stone, etc.

Preparation:
Cover tables with newspaper.
Cut paper to approximately 20 × 30 cm.
Children to mix the paint to a creamy consistency, see notes on page 155.
Give out the other materials.

Introduction:
Ask the children to look closely at the object in front of them and to say what they notice about it. What colours are there? Does it smell or taste of anything? What does it feel like with the eyes closed?
Can they describe the texture? What words could we use?
Invite the children to make a painting that describes how the surface of their object feels.
Note: *not* a picture of their object. If they wish, children may add the gritty substances to their paint jar, or they could sprinkle some on to their painting before the paint is dry.

Development:
If the paint is really thick and creamy, the children should gain great satisfaction in building up one colour on to another, so that the surface of the painting derives its own textural quality. Natural or local colour is not important and it is unlikely that the results will be realistic in any way. The value of this exercise comes from the handling of the paint and the unexpected results when colours merge and mix.
Try to keep the colours in the jars clean by encouraging the children to always wash and dry the brush before dipping it into a different colour.

Evaluation:
Did the children enjoy this session?
Did the paintings suggest the roughness of the surfaces?
Were there any unexpected results?

Activity: Painting fish.

Concept: Colour/shape/pattern.

Aim: To make children aware of the
                      main features of fish.
                      To use colour more
                      imaginatively.

                      See Colour Plate F

Resources   1. Newspaper; any cheap paper; water jars, one between two; paint rags, one each; the
needed: primary colours plus black and white paint; brushes.
                      2. Pictures and slides of colourful fish.
                      3. Slide projector.

Preparation: Set up projector.
                      Cut paper into a variety of sizes.
                      Cover the table with newspaper, mix paints and give out materials.

Introduction: Show slides of tropical fish, pointing out the fish's main features: shape, tail, fins, eyes,
                      mouth, patterns, scales, colour.
                      Discuss pictures of fish in books and ask some children to describe them in terms of the above
                      features.

Development: Ask children either to paint a picture of a fish that they have seen, or to invent one that no-
                      one else has seen.
                      Remind them how to keep the paints clean by washing and drying the brush before dipping it
                      into a fresh colour.
                      Remind them of some of the features that *all* fish have.
                      Ask them what else they might include in their pictures – ferns, seaweed, sand, stones, etc.

Evaluation: Did the children handle the paint with skill?
                      Were they able to express fish shapes and add relevant details?

Activity:	Wave patterns.
Concept:	Colour/rhythm.
Aim:	To encourage colour mixing. To stimulate interest in the movement of water.

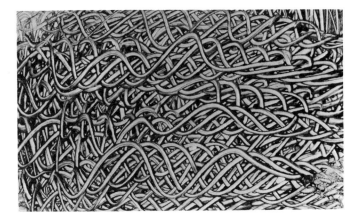

Resources needed:
1. Finger paints, see notes on page 164; shiny paper, glossy magazines with no pictures; cardboard combs; newspapers.
2. Pictures of the sea, photographs and artists' impressions; records of wave noises; any sea poems, e.g. 'The Sea' by James Reeves, 'Seascape' by W.H. Auden.

Preparation: Cover tables with newspapers, make cardboard combs and give out materials.

Introduction: Read the sea poems and listen to the record of wave sounds. Refer to the rhythm of the waves. Show the pictures and discuss the patterns made by waves, using words like swirling, rippling, crashing, rushing, etc. Discuss sea colours and how they might be mixed from the colours available.
Demonstrate comb painting. Put about a teaspoonful of paint on to the shiny paper and spread it with fingers and/or cardboard comb. Suggest how wave patterns might be formed. Extra colours may be added and mixed in.

Development: Play the record again while the children are working and encourage them to make wave noises at the same time.
Those who do not enjoy getting messy could make paper or string collages.
Discuss results.

Evaluation: Did the children mix appropriate colours?
Did the final results suggest the movement of waves?

Activity: Fish from texture rubbings.

Concept: Pattern/texture.

Aim: To show how texture rubbings may be used to represent a patterned surface.
To make children more aware of the patterns made by fish scales.

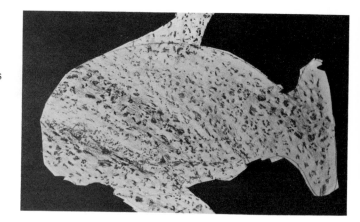

Resources needed:
1. Any thin, tough paper, duplicating paper, etc.; wax crayons; backing paper; scissors; glue.
2. A real fish or possibly a stuffed fish.
3. Any textured surface with an even pattern that could be rubbed to simulate fish scales.

Preparation: Cut paper to about 20 × 30 cm.
Display the results of Session 15.

Introduction: Discuss the results of Session 15.
Show the fish and talk about its scales. Point out that they repeat the same shape over and over again, which we call a pattern.
Show the pattern with the textured surface and demonstrate how to make a texture rubbing by placing some paper over it, holding it steady then rubbing firmly with wax crayons.

Development: Suggest that the children might like to find their own textures round the school in order to make rubbings from them.
When they have completely covered their paper with rubbings, ask them to draw a fish shape that nearly fills the paper. Cut away the background and mount on to a contrasting sheet of paper, either individually or as a group frieze.

Evaluation: Did the children enjoy this?
Did the finished results indicate that they had learned anything about the shape, pattern and texture of a fish?

Activity: Undersea collage.

Concept: Colour/shape.

Aim: To allow experimentation with collage materials.
To stimulate an imaginative response. To encourage mixing of appropriate colours.

Resources needed:
1. Newspaper; any cheap, white paper; water jars, one between two; paint rags, one each; yellow, blue, white, black, turquoise or sea green paint; large brushes; jars for paint; mixing palettes, one each; paste; scissors; offcuts of paper suitable for seaweed, rocks, etc.
2. Pictures of life under the sea. Any poems connected with life under the sea.

Preparation: Cut paper to approximately 40 × 30 cm. Cover tables with newspaper. Mix thick, creamy paint and give out materials. Display the results of Session 17.

Introduction: Briefly refer to the results of Session 17. Read the poems and discuss the undersea pictures, paying particular attention to the colours found in the water and the types and shape of seaweed. Discuss how the children might mix the sea colours from the available paints. Ask the children to imagine that they were sitting on the sea bed. What would they notice?

Development: Invite the children to mix some sea colours in their palettes and to cover their paper. They might keep to one colour or they may try several. Remind children to wash and dry their brushes before dipping into a clean colour.
When the paint is fairly dry, they may add any other details by sticking cut or torn paper shapes.

Evaluation: Did the children mix appropriate colours?
Were they able to express underwater life with collage materials?

Activity: Undersea monster – drawings/ paintings/collage.

Concept: Colour/pattern/texture.

Aim: To encourage an imaginative response.
To allow experimentation with materials.

Resources needed:
1. Newspaper; any cheap paper; water jars; paint rags; paints; brushes; palettes; glue; colour magazines; paper offcuts; crayons.
2. Pictures of prehistoric creatures and strangely exotic underwater creatures.

Preparation: Cut paper to a variety of sizes.
Cover tables with newspaper and give out materials.

Introduction: Tell the children about the Loch Ness monster and of any other strange creatures that live on the ocean bed, that no-one has ever seen. Ask if the children could imagine what they might look like. Invite suggestions.
Show some of the pictures and discuss features not normally found on animals that we know. Invite children to invent their own monster that no-one has ever seen. They may use any of the materials, either singly or combined, e.g. crayon and paint, paint with collage materials, etc.

Development: While work is in progress, children should be encouraged to consider details such as texture and pattern on the creatures' skin. Remind them of previous sessions on pattern and texture. If there is time, suggest that the children might like to put in some seaweed, rocks, etc.

Evaluation: Were the results imaginative?
Were there any unexpected results?

Activity: Easter bonnets.

Concept: Shape/colour/pattern

Aim: To improve manipulative
                  skills. To encourage selection
                  and discrimination.

Resources   1. Sugar paper; tissue paper; feathers; patterned wallpaper samples; water jars; paint rags;
needed: paints; palettes; scissors; PVA adhesive.
                 2. Pictures of fancy hats or bonnets of different shapes. Try to get photographs of an Easter
                    bonnet parade or Ascot.

Preparation: Cut paper to approximately 20 × 30 cm. Cover tables with newspaper. Give out painting
                  materials and paper.

Introduction: Show children the pictures of hats and talk about the Easter bonnet parades. Invite them to
                  paint a hat in their favourite colour so that it almost fills the paper. Do not bother to draw it
                  first, but think about its shape and then fill it in.

Development: When the paint is dry tell the children to cut out their bonnet. They may then decorate it
                  with feathers, little pieces of tissue paper screwed up to suggest flowers, or parts of patterns cut
                  from the wallpaper. Tell them not to stick things down immediately, but to cut most of their
                  decorations out first. This will give you a chance to advise them about the work before it is
                  too late to do anything about it. Advice, however, should be based on discussion about
                  choice of colours, how much to put on or leave off, spacing things out, etc.

Evaluation: Did the children enjoy this session?
                  Were they able to handle the painting, cutting out and gluing tasks successfully?
                  Were the children pleased with the results?

Activity: Exploring clay.

Concept: Form/texture.

Aim: To introduce children to clay and to explore its expressive possibilities.

Resources needed:
1. Clay; newspaper; damp cloth or plastic bag.
2. Items that will make a mark when pressed into clay: pencils, cotton reels, screws, etc.

Preparation: Cover tables with newspaper.
Prepare clay so that each child has a ball about the size of a small orange.
Keep the clay covered with a damp rag or in a plastic bag, until it is needed as it very quickly dries out.

Introduction: Give out the clay and tell the children that they can pinch, squeeze, pull, poke holes in it or roll it, but that they must not break pieces off. The clay must remain *whole*.
This activity will probably generate lots of excitement and the teacher should encourage the children to discuss the shapes they are making.

Development: When the initial excitement has decreased, the teacher might invite the children to press the clay back to its original spherical shape and ask if the children can make other forms: e.g. ovoid (egg), cylinder (fat worm), cube, etc, but still keeping the clay in one piece.
Finally the children should press out on the desk pancake shapes, about 1 cm thick. Tell them to turn it over, so that the flat side is uppermost, and to see what marks can be made with the items provided.
If the clay starts to crack because it is drying out, it is better to stop at that point, or progress to Session 22 using a fresh ball of clay. See page 158 for hints on keeping clay.

Evaluation: Did the children enjoy this activity?
Were they able to make the simple forms suggested?
Were there any unexpected outcomes?

Activity: Modelling in clay.

Concept: Form/texture.

Aim: To provide the opportunity to
explore the expressive qualities
of clay.

Resources needed:

1. Clay; newspaper; damp cloth or plastic bag; overalls; lolly sticks, sharpened twigs, etc. that will serve as modelling tools.
2. Pictures of animals that do not have long, thin limbs or bodies and are preferably textured or patterned, such as tortoise, hedgehog, hampster, etc.

Preparation: Cover tables with newspaper.
Prepare the clay so that each child has a ball about the size of a small orange.
Keep the clay covered with a damp rag, or in a plastic bag, until it is needed, as it very quickly dries out.

Introduction: Show children the pictures and discuss shape, texture, and pattern.
Remind the children of Session 21. Tell them that they must keep the clay in one piece again and should roll or pinch the clay to make the basic shape of their chosen animal. Details, such as nose, ears, etc. should be pinched into shape. Finally, any markings or texture may be added with the modelling tools.

Development: Clay should be allowed to dry slowly and may take a week to dry thoroughly. Dry clay is extremely brittle and should be handled with utmost care. For this reason it is not advisable for young children to decorate their models. If firing the models is out of the question (see Session 120) they can be strengthened by dipping or coating thoroughly in PVA. Teachers might feel inclined, however, to treat these exploratory efforts as being ephemeral and, after a period on display they could be reduced back to clay to be re-used. See page 158.

Evaluation: Were the children able to make the basic shape of their animal?
Were they able to add appropriate texturing?

Activity: Radial designs using wax resist.

Concept: Pattern/line.

Aim: To make children aware of radial patterns.
To teach children the principle of wax resist.

Resources needed:

1. Light-coloured wax crayons; white paper or card; dark, runny dye or paint (dye, e.g. *Brusho*, is much more successful); newspaper; brushes; paint jars.
2. Anything circular to be used as a template.
3. Examples of radial designs, e.g. wheels, daisy, etc.

Preparation: Cover desks with newspaper.
Mix dye or paint, then test it by brushing over some crayoned lines to ensure that the crayons do, in fact, resist the paint. If the paint is too thick and covers the crayon, dilute it. It should, however, not be so watery that it does not contrast in tone with the crayon.
Cut paper into squares approximately 15 × 15 cm and if necessary cut these into a circle and mark a dot in the centre.

Introduction: Show examples of radial designs and explain how lines radiate from the centre. Ask for other examples of this.
Demonstrate the wax resist technique by making a few lines with crayon, pressing heavily, and then brushing over lightly with runny paint or dye.

Development: Ask the children to draw a circle, make a dot in the middle, then design their own radial pattern using only lines and pressing heavily on their crayons. Remind them of lines used previously; dotty, wiggly, etc. Their second attempt might be an imaginary flower. Finally, dark paint or dye is brushed over the designs to enhance the colour, and the circles cut out.

Evaluation: Did the results indicate that the children had understood the principles of wax resist and radial patterns?
Were there any imaginative results?

Activity: Group project – huge creature

Concept: Pattern/texture.

Aim: To consolidate concepts learned in previous sessions. To improve manipulative skills.

Resources needed: Stiff paper or thin card, preferably dark; PVA adhesive and spatulas; circular objects for drawing round, approximately 10 cm diameter; wool and string offcuts; any small items that could be stuck down in lines, e.g. beads, buttons, lentils, etc.

Preparation: Ask the children to bring in some small items for sticking down.
Display work from Session 23.
Cut the paper into squares approximately 15 × 15 cm.
Distribute materials.

Introduction: Discuss the work done during Session 23. Remind the children that the designs were made by drawing lines from the centre of the circle. This Session the radial designs will be made by sticking things to the paper, starting from the centre again and working towards the edge in straight lines.
Demonstrate how this might be done with pieces of string or wool cut to size beforehand. As an alternative, show how lines of beads, buttons or lentils could achieve a similar effect.

Development: The children start by drawing and cutting out their circle. Put a dot in the centre and make radials by painting a line of adhesive from the dot to the edge of the circle and sticking things down.
Discuss other ways in which radial designs could be made, then make some.
The designs might be displayed as the skin of a multi-coloured imaginary creature, or perhaps the children could think of another idea.

Evaluation: Did the children remember how to make a radial design?
Were there any novel suggestions for producing radial designs?

Activity: Planet project using slides.

Concept: Line.

Aim: To teach fine finger movements.
To stimulate the children's interest through projected images.

Resources needed:
1. Slide projector and screen; old 35 mm slides or plastic slide holders and acetate or clear film; black paint; liquid soap (washing-up liquid); pins; scissors.
2. Preferably a darkened room or corridor. If this is out of the question, slides could be projected against a white wall under a table by a window.
3. Slides and/or photographs of outer space.
4. Recording of *The Planets* by Holst and a record player.

Preparation: Set up the projector and screen.
Mix half a cup of black paint to a creamy consistency and add a teaspoonful of liquid soap. Use this to paint the dull surface of the old slides. Alternatively paint some clear film black. When dry, cut it up to fit into the plastic slide holders.

Introduction: Show the children the slides and photographs of outer space. Refer particularly to the number of stars and planets, the colours noticed, the blackness of space, etc.
Play excerpts from *The Planets* by Holst and any other appropriate music.
Explain that the children will make their own slide of outer space. Demonstrate on a prepared piece of acetate or old slide. With a pin, scissors or any other sharp instrument, scratch away tiny circles or make pin pricks. Mistakes can be quickly covered with a little of the soapy paint, and then scratched some more.
Hand out the prepared slides.

Development: When a child has finished scratching his slide, project it immediately, then, if necessary some more stars or planets can be added to it. By way of a presentation, the teacher might collect up all the slides and project them whilst playing some appropriate musical accompaniment.

Evaluation: Did the children enjoy this Session?
Was there much discussion about the slides?
Were there any unexpected results?

Activity: Planet project – paintings.

Concept: Colour.

Aim: To consolidate previous work on colour mixing and the wax resist technique. To arouse children's interest in outer space.

Resources needed:
1. Newspaper; any cheap white paper; water jars, one between two; paint rags, one each; the primary colours plus black and white; brushes; palettes; scissors; pencils, crayons, circular objects approximately 20 cm in diameter.
2. Photographs of planets; recording of *The Planets* by Holst.

Preparation: Cut paper to approximately 40 × 30 cm.
Cover tables with newspaper.
Mix paints and give out painting materials.

Introduction: Remind children of the slides that they made during the previous Session. Show them photographs of planets and discuss the colours.
Suggest that they might like to paint their own planet but using only tints and shades of one colour. Demonstrate how to draw a circle by tracing round a circular object. The children start by drawing a circle that almost fills their paper and then painting it. Holst's music playing quietly in the background might help to provide a suitable atmosphere.

Development: While their painting is drying suggest that they draw stars with wax crayons on a second piece of paper. When finished the whole of the paper is brushed over *lightly* with black dye or runny black paint. Finally, children cut out their planet and stick it on to their starry sky.

Evaluation: Did the children mix tints and shades properly?
Did they remember about wax resist?
Was there much comment about space?
Did the children enjoy listening to the music while they were working?

Activity:	Planet project – texture collage.
Concept:	Texture.

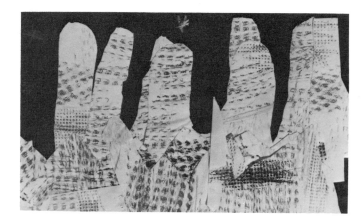

Aim:	To encourage an imaginative response. To allow practise with collage techniques.
Resources needed:	1. Thin, fairly tough white paper for rubbings; wax crayons; paste; scissors; chalk; black paper approximately 20 × 30 cm. 2. Record of *The Planets* by Holst, music from *2001*, *Star Wars*, etc. 3. Photographs of the moon's surface.
Preparation:	Display the results of the previous Session. Display some of the photographs of the moon's surface. Cut the white paper to approximately 15 × 10 cm and give each child about six pieces. Give out crayons.
Introduction:	Refer to the display of work. This is the view that a spaceman would have coming to land on the planet. Refer to the photographs of the moon's surface and ask the children if their planet would have the same sort of surface. Remind the children how they did texture rubbings (Session 17), then ask them to make some from surfaces around the school. These will be used for the surface of their planet.
Development:	Tell the children to cut or tear their texture rubbings to make a picture of the surface of their planet. Arrange all the shapes before sticking down. If any sky is showing, stars could be added with chalk. Ask the children if they would like to listen to some 'space' music while they worked.
Evaluation:	Was there much discussion about the surface of their planet? Were they able to respond imaginatively?

Activity:	Planet project – three-dimensional landscapes.
Concept:	Texture/form.
Aim:	To encourage the expressive use of Plasticine or clay. To consolidate previous work done in clay.

Resources needed: Plasticine or clay; cardboard or hardboard bases, approximately 15 × 15 cm; twigs, pencils, etc. for texturing the models.

Preparation: Display the results of Session 27.
Give each child a small ball of clay and a baseboard.

Introduction: Discuss the work of the previous Session. Ask the children to imagine what they would see as they walked about on the planet. Can they describe what the rocks would feel like, how tall they are, what shape they are, etc.
Suggest that the children might like to make the surface of their planet from Plasticine or clay by pressing it on to rough surfaces and by scratching or poking it with twigs or pencils.

Development: The children start by making a fairly flat base to which more Plasticine or clay is added to suggest hills and rocks. These could be textured by the methods demonstrated, or by any others that the children might invent.
Encourage a variety of textures and levels, with perhaps caves or tunnels.

Evaluation: Did the models suggest the surface texture of a planet?
Were there any unusual or original results?

Activity: Planet creature – paint/collage.

Concept: Colour/texture.

Aim: To encourage an imaginative response.
To consolidate previous work on colour mixing and collage.

Resources needed:
1. Newspaper; any cheap paper; water jars, one between two; paint rags, one each; the primary colours plus black and white; brushes; palettes; chalk; string, wool, textured paper, etc.; PVA adhesive.
2. Any poems about imaginary or unusual creatures, e.g. Edward Lear's 'The Jumblies', 'The Akond of Swat', 'The Yonghy Bonghy Bo', or James Reeves' Prefabulous Animiles (a collection of verses). Pictures of animals that have rough-textured skins; crocodiles, lizards, etc.

Preparation: Display the results of Sessions 27 and 28.
Cut paper to approximately 40 × 30 cm.
Cover tables with newspaper, mix paints and give out materials.

Introduction: Read the poems about imaginary animals. Show the pictures of real animals and discuss the texture of their skin. Ask children for words to describe how it would feel.
Refer to the children's work of Sessions 27 and 28 and suggest they paint a picture of a creature that lives on their planet. For camouflage reasons its skin might be textured using string or any other suitable collage materials.

Development: Ask the children to draw an outline of their creature with chalk, so that it almost fills their paper, then to stick on materials for its textured skin. Finally, tints and shades of their chosen colour should be mixed and painted over the whole of the creature.
Alternatively, some children might prefer to cut or tear their colours from magazine pictures, and fill in their outline with these instead of using paint.
For display purposes, the teacher might prefer to cut out the creatures and re-mount them.

Evaluation: Were the children able to mix appropriate tints and shades?
Did their creatures appear to have textured skins?
Were any of the results highly imaginative?

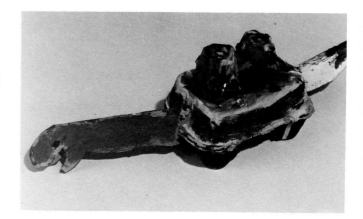

Activity:　　　　Planet creature – models.

Concept:　　　　Form/colour.

Aim:　　　　To introduce a model-making
technique.
To use colour expressively.

**Resources
needed:**　　　Cardboard egg boxes; sugar paper; water jars; paint rags; the primary colours plus black and
white paint; palettes; scissors; PVA adhesive; newspaper.

Preparation:　　Cover the tables with newspaper.
Give out egg boxes, sugar paper, scissors and PVA.
Display the results of Session 29.

Introduction:　　Refer to the results of Session 29. Ask the children what their creature is like: frightening,
timid, fierce, etc. Which ones look the most ferocious, and why? Suggest that they might like
to make some really ferocious creatures for their planet, using egg boxes for the body and sugar
paper for the head and tail. Demonstrate how to make the head and tail by folding a strip of
sugar paper in half, lengthways. These are attached to the body by cutting slits into the egg
boxes.

Development:　　When children have made their basic shape as demonstrated, encourage them to add
features, by cutting other egg boxes and sticking pieces to the creatures.
Finally, the children should paint their creature, using bright, frightening colours.

Evaluation:　　Did the children enjoy this session?
Did the results evoke discussion?
Did the children think their creatures looked fierce?

Activity: Drawing leaves.

Concept: Line.

Aim: To make the children aware of line in nature.
To increase children's powers of observation and concentration.

Resources needed:
1. Pencils; felt-tip pens; ball-point pens; any cheap white paper; dark mounting paper; scissors; chalk.
2. Large leaves with clearly defined lines.

Preparation: Flatten leaves by placing them between newspaper under heavy books. Cut the white paper to about 10 × 15 cm. Let the children choose a drawing implement.

Introduction: Give each child a leaf. Ask what they notice about it. Discuss its colour, shape, texture and refer to the patterns made by the veins. Notice the position and angle of the veins in relation to the stem. What is the outline of the leaf like? Is it perfectly smooth or serrated?

Development: A leaf is placed in the centre of the white paper, held steady, and the outline is lightly drawn in chalk. With this outline to help them, the children are then invited to add all the fine detail that they can see, using their chosen drawing implement. The chalk can be removed by rubbing with a soft cloth. These drawings may be trimmed and mounted against the dark paper or put into a class folder.

Evaluation: What was the response to the introduction?
Did the children work enthusiastically?
For how long did they concentrate on drawing?
Did the finished results indicate that they had closely observed the leaf?

Activity:	Painting trees.
Concept:	Colour.
Aim:	To explore the qualities of paint further. To express an experience through painting.

Resources needed:	1. Newspaper; any cheap paper; water jars, one between two; paint rags, one each; primary colours and black and white paints; paint brushes; palettes. 2. Pictures of trees.
Preparation:	Display pictures of trees. Cut paper to different sizes. Cover tables with newspaper and give out materials.
Introduction:	Refer to the pictures of trees and ask the children to describe any recent expeditions to woods or parks. What did they notice about the trees? What colours were the leaves, trunk, etc. Remind the children how to mix their colours without making the colours in the jars dirty. (See Session 15).
Development:	Without any previous drawing, ask the children to paint a picture that includes trees. Ask them to think about the colours and to mix them in their palette. This could be a picture of something that they have done, or it could be purely imaginary. Ask them to choose a piece of paper that they know they will fill. Discuss some of the results, referring to any unusual mixtures of colours.
Evaluation:	Did the children handle the paint skilfully? Could they mix the required colours? Could they express simple ideas through their painting?

Activity: Halloween models.

Concept: Form/colour

Aim: To introduce children to a
                     model-making technique.
                     To stimulate an imaginative
                     response.

Resources   1. Empty washing-up liquid bottles; cardboard tubes; newspaper; tissue paper; black sugar
needed: paper; offcuts of wool or string for hair; PVA adhesive; scissors; sticky tape.
                    2. Photographs of witches, poems or stories about witches and Halloween.

Preparation: Display the witch pictures.
                    Ask children to supply empty washing-up liquid bottles and any black material suitable for a
                    witch's clothing.

Introduction: Read the poems and stories connected with Halloween. Ask the children how they would
                    recognise a witch if they met one. What things would they notice about her?
                    Demonstrate how to make a cloaked figure starting with a washing-up liquid bottle. Make a
                    ball of newspaper for the head and stick it to the top of the bottle with tape. This is the basic
                    shape. Demonstrate how to make a cone-shaped hat by cutting a circle from black paper,
                    then cutting a radius line and folding the paper into a cone.

Development: When the children have made their basic figure shape, as explained, tell them to cover the
                    newspaper with tissue paper for the face, and to stick this down with more tape. They can
                    then add facial features with cut-out paper, string or wool for the hair, etc. The witch's cloak
                    and skirt could be made from black paper or any fabric offcuts available.
                    Encourage the children to make their own witch, who will not look like any other witch. Ask
                    them what is different about their witch.

Evaluation: What was the children's response to the poems and stories?
                    Did they attempt to make individual responses, or did they just copy one another?
                    Did the children handle the materials properly?

Activity: Red display.

Concept: Colour.

Aim: To make the children aware of the different reds that exist in their environment.
To demonstrate that a colour can vary in tone.

Resources needed: As many different *red* backing materials as can be found; paper, Cellophane, tissue paper, crepe paper, etc.
Any red objects.
Reproductions of paintings or magazine photographs where red is the predominant colour.
As many different plain red papers or material as possible, cut to the same size, about 15 × 20 cm.

Preparation: Prepare the table with a display board behind, preferably in the classroom.
Cover all surfaces with red paper or material, ready for the children's offerings. Ask the children to bring in things from home that are *entirely* red, and to put them on the table.
Display the reproductions and photographs.

Introduction: Ask the children to talk about the things brought from home and ask questions aimed at increasing their understanding of red: What colour is it? Can you see something else on the display or in the room that is the same shade of red? Is John's red car lighter or darker than Susan's red skirt? Can you count the number of different reds? etc.

Development: Ask the children to rearrange the things on display so that the objects are in groups of the same shade of red. Put the lightest reds on one end of the table and the darkest on the opposite end. Do the same with the red papers so that you have a tonal scale going from light to dark. Children could work individually or in groups.
Ask them to think of names for all the different reds so that they can identify them e.g. tomato, pillar box, blood, etc. Label the objects on display with these names.

Evaluation: Did the display generate interest?
Did the introduction spark off plenty of discussion?
Were the children able to make a tonal scale of reds?

Activity: Collage in red.

Concept: Colour.

Aim: To consolidate work done during the previous Session. To build up skill in handling paint and collage materials.

See Colour Plate R

Resources needed:
1. Newspaper; any cheap, white paper; water jars, one between two; paint rags, one each; red, white and black paints (if possible have more than one red e.g., crimson and vermilion); brushes; palettes; paste, scraps of paper, material, etc., suitable for collage.
2. Any poems about colours, particularly *red*.

Preparation: Cut paper to approximately 30 × 20 cm.
Cover tables with newspaper and give out materials.

Introduction: Read the poems. Refer to the display, and remind the children of the different reds that exist. Invite the children to make a painting or collage, or combination of both, that shows lots of different reds.

Development: Ask the children to make a dot near the middle of their paper and to start by painting or sticking a circle. Go round with more circles but change the red each time. Keep going until every bit of the paper is coloured red. Remind the children to vary the tones so that the design has some light and dark parts.
Discuss the results. Who has the darkest red in their picture? Who has more than ten reds? Who has mixed the same red as something on the display? Check by holding the painting against it.

Evaluation: Were a good range of reds mixed?
Did the designs have contrast of tone in them?
Could the children handle the collage materials?

Activity: Painting a stripy draggon.

Concept: Colour.

Aim: To increase awareness of the colour red.
To consolidate introduction to tints and shades.

See Colour Plate G

Resources needed:
1. Newspaper; any cheap, white paper; water jars, one between two; paint rags, one each; red, white and black paints; large brushes; jars for paint, three to a group; mixing palettes, one each. If possible more than one red, e.g. crimson and vermilion.
2. Short story about a dragon.
3. Frieze paper or similar, scissors.

Preparation: Cut off a length of frieze paper and cut paper approximately 20 × 15 cm.
Cover tables with newspaper.
One-third fill jars with thick creamy paint and give out materials.

Introduction: Read the story about a dragon. Tell your own story of a light pink dragon who used to blow out fire and went gradually darker when he did so. What do the children imagine this dragon looked like? Invite descriptions. Encourage someone to draw an outline in chalk on the frieze paper.
Divide the class into three groups. About one-third will paint shades of red and two-thirds will paint tints of red. Draw chalk lines on the dragon so that every child has a stripe to fill in.

Development: Each child will mix one tint or shade and paint a strip on the edge of their small piece of paper, then cut it. Encourage a full range of tints and shades. Have the children lay out the strips and, after discussion, see if they can arrange them in a tonal scale. The lightest and darkest should be at opposite ends. Using this as a guide, get them to paint the dragon with the same colours and in the same order.
Remind the child of the previous Sessions and how to keep the colours clean.

Evaluation: Could they remember how to make a tint or a shade?
Could they arrange their strips in a tonal scale?
Did they enjoy the end result?

Activity: Dragon models.

Concept: Form/colour.

Aim: To introduce a model-
                  making technique.
                  To use colour expressively.

Resources needed: Newspaper, popular tabloid size; wallpaper paste; large brushes; string or elastic bands; gum strip or sticky tape; water jars; paint rags; the primary colours plus black and white; palettes.

Preparation: Display the results of Session 36.
                    Tear newspapers into single sheets, four per child. Mix up paste and paint.

Introduction: Refer to the results of Session 36. Ask the children what the dragon is like – frightening, timid, fierce, etc. Suggest that they might like to make their own dragon.
Demonstrate how to build a simple base with rolled newspaper.
1. Roll, as tightly as possible, one sheet of newspaper and stick in about five places with gum strip or tape. Repeat this until you have three similar rolls.
2. Place them side by side and tie them together in the middle or place an elastic band around them.
3. Bend the newspaper to give a rough skeleton shape of an animal.
4. Tear up a sheet of newspaper to pieces approximately 5 × 3 cm.
5. Paste the rolled newspaper thoroughly and stick on the small pieces, one at a time, overlapping slightly. Go over with more paste until the newspaper is reasonably flat.

Development: Tell the children to paint their models, after they have dried, to try to make them look fierce.

Evaluation: Did the children enjoy this Session?
                   Did the results evoke discussion?
                   Did the children think their creatures were fierce?

Activity: Bonfire models.

Concept: Colour/form.

Aim: To improve observation.
                    To encourage the use of
                    appropriate colours and
                    materials.
                    To allow practice at expressing
                    an idea three-dimensionally.

Resources   Cardboard or hardboard offcuts approximately 20 × 30 cm; blocks of polystyrene made from
needed: discarded packaging; twigs; PVA adhesive; any materials that would add texture to the
                    baseboard – sand, sawdust, etc.; newspapers; painting materials; matches; candle; bowl of
                    water.

Preparation: Make a large taper by rolling up a piece of newspaper. Cut polystyrene blocks roughly into
                    cylinders approximately 5 cm high. Cover tables with newspaper.

Introduction: Ask the children which colours they have seen in flames. Light a candle and ask the same
                    question. Blow it out, light the taper and discuss the different colours and shapes made by the
                    flames. Extinguish it by dropping it into the bowl of water.

Development: Invite the children to make a bonfire model with the flames leaping into the air.
                    Children could use a block of polystyrene stuck to a piece of cardboard as a base for their
                    bonfire. Twigs could be pushed into it and painted with appropriate colours.
                    As an addition to twigs, children might use paper dipped into paste, or muslin strips dipped
                    into runny plaster of Paris or Polyfilla.
                    The baseboard could be textured by coating it with PVA adhesive and then adding sawdust,
                    sand, grass cuttings, etc.
                    Finally, little clay or Plasticine figures could be added to the scene.

Evaluation: Did the results indicate that the children had observed the colours and shapes of flames?
                    Were the children able to express the character of a bonfire?

Activity: A firework display.

Concept: Colour/line.

Aim: To encourage the inventive
                       use of colour and line.
                       To introduce new ways of
                       making lines.

**Resources   Black or dark paper; cartridge paper or any non-absorbent paper; coloured inks or runny
needed:**   paint; drinking straws; newspaper.

Preparation: Mix up the paint and test it for straw blowing. The paint should run freely across the paper
                  when it is being blown.

Introduction: Ask children to describe their favourite firework. Invite them to invent a new firework.
                  Demonstrate straw blowing. Put a generous blob of ink or runny paint on to the paper. Put
                  one end of a drinking straw about 1 cm away from the blob and blow into the other end,
                  causing the colour to scatter in zig-zag lines. Keep blowing the lines across the paper until the
                  colour runs out.

Development: This technique could be used to form a background to a bonfire scene, with rockets bursting
                  in the sky.

Evaluation: Did the results suggest fireworks?
                  Were there any unusual results?

Activity:	A Christmas picture	
Concept:	Shape/pattern.	
Aim:	To make children more aware of patterns on our clothes. To encourage an individual response to a story. To allow practice at cutting shapes.	

Resources needed:

1. Any fairly dark backing paper; wallpaper sample book; scissors; paste and spatulas; pencils; sugar paper.
2. Poems or stories about the visit of the angels to the shepherds, e.g. The Nativity in the New Testament, 'Shepherd's Tale' by Steven Ponchon.

Preparation: Cover a display board or cupboard door with the backing paper.
Cut the sugar paper to approximately 20 × 30 cm.

Introduction: Read the poems and stories, then suggest to the children that they draw a simple outline of an angel so that it fills their piece of sugar paper. The children could either decorate the angel's gown with crayons or paint, or cut suitable patterns from the wallpapers. You might even suggest the same colour scheme for all the angels. When complete, the angels should be cut out ready for placing on the background.

Development: As children finish, the angels could be pinned on to the backing sheet, perhaps with Gabriel in a slightly more prominent position, then finally stuck down.
Alternatively the angels could be used as the design for Christmas cards or calendars.

Evaluation: How did the children respond to the stories?
Did the children choose their patterns carefully, and perhaps discuss the suitability of certain patterns and colours?
Did they manage to cut out shapes that fitted their pencil outline?

Activity:	Taking a line for a walk by chance – a game.
Concept:	Line.
Aim:	To develop skill in hand-to-eye movement further.

Resources needed: Pencils; fibre-tip or ball-point pens; graph paper with 1 cm squares.

Preparation: Cut graph paper to approximately 20 × 30 cm. Ask children to choose one drawing instrument. Make two spinners – one with numbers one to eight; the other with left, right, up, down.

Introduction: Explain that they are going to take a line for a walk over the graph paper. They must stay on the lines and go the way the spinning tops say e.g. if the first spinner lands on six and the other on up, then the children draw a line upwards for six squares, and so on.

Development: The children take it in turns to spin the tops and call out to the others what they say. In this way all the drawings will be different. With the exception of the first caller, tell the children to put their pen or pencil on a line near the centre of their paper.
When everyone has had a turn at calling, or the drawings have filled the paper, tell the children to colour in the shapes with different colours.

Evaluation: Did the children enjoy this session?
Did they manage to follow the instructions of the caller and keep to the lines?

Activity: Discovering shapes.

Concept: Line/shape.

Aim: To develop skill in handling drawing implements.
To make children aware that lines enclose shapes.

Resources needed: Crayons; pencils; fibre-tip, felt-tip and ball-point pens; any cheap, light-coloured paper.

Preparation: Cut the paper to about 20 × 30 cm.
Ask children to choose any drawing implement.
Display results of Session 41.

Introduction: Remind the children of Session 41 and how their lines explored the paper. This Session they will take another line for a walk, but over plain paper. They must start and finish at the same place, and walk their line all over the paper, but this time they don't have to go in straight lines. They can invent their own path, but the pen or pencil must not lift off the paper until it has returned to its starting point. Lines may cross over or avoid one another.

Development: Tell the children not to rush, and to think where their line is going and what sort of path it is taking. When they have finished ask them to turn their paper round and round slowly and see if their lines have made shapes that they can recognise. There might be a fish, a bird or flower. If they can see something, colour it in and colour the rest of the paper with black crayon so that the shape stands out clearly. Or cut it out and stick it on to a contrasting background. If no recognisable shapes emerge, colour in the shapes made by the line to make an abstract design. Allow time to discuss the finished results.

Evaluation: Did the children enjoy this Session?
Were many different types of lines invented?
Did all of the children produce either an abstract design or colour in the shape of something perceived in their line drawing?

Activity: Collage – predators

Concept: Texture/shape/colour.

Aim: To encourage children to
                accurately observe and express
                the shape, colour and texture
                of an actual creature.

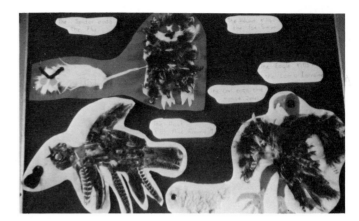

Resources   1. Sugar paper; scissors; PVA adhesive and spatulas; chalk; a great variety of collage materials
needed: that will express the surface texture of animals, birds, fish, etc.
                2. Books and photographs of animals, birds, fish, insects, etc.

Preparation: Sort out the collage materials into separate piles or boxes (see notes on waste materials on
                page 160).
                Cut paper to approximately 20 × 30 cm and 20 × 15 cm.

Introduction: Ask the children to think of all the animals that chase and kill other animals. Make a list on
                the board and discuss. Introduce the word predator.
                Suggest that the children work in pairs – one child making the predator, the other its prey.
                Tell the children to find a picture of their chosen creature.

Development: Small creatures should be sketched in chalk to almost fill the small pieces of sugar paper.
                Large creatures should fill the larger sheets.
                Children should then stick on their collage materials, trying to convey the characteristics of
                the creatures, colouring and texture.
                When finished, the two creatures could either be cut out and mounted with a caption, e.g.
                'the spider kills the fly', or they could be cut out and stuck to another sheet. In which case the
                children could work in pairs on the background, probably with paints or crayon.

Evaluation: Did the children manage to express the chief characteristics of their creature?
                Were the materials used imaginatively and handled with skill?
                Did the children enjoy this Session?

Activity: Making simple booklets.

Concept: That designs sometimes have a utilitarian purpose.

Aim: To introduce simple bookcraft techniques.

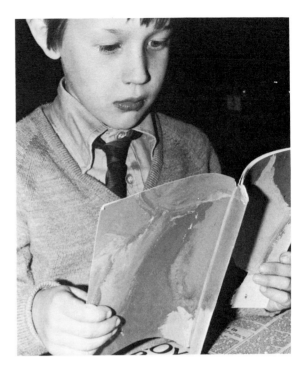

Resources needed: Each child will need:
1. About three pieces of duplicating paper or similar for pages; scissors; a strip of strawboard, 1 cm wide, the length should be the same as the width of your paper; piece of string or wool, three times the length of the cardboard strip (a large elastic band could be used).
2. A design for the cover – this could be the result of Session 42, or any other design made previously.

Preparation: Give out materials.

Introduction: Explain that everyone will make a booklet, and ask each child what it would like it to be used for.

Development: Cut out the cover to the same size as the pages.
Fold each page in half. Fold the cover in half, then interleave them so that the cover is on the outside. Put the card strip in the centre of the booklet, running along the crease.
With the booklet closed and the card forming the spine, mark the position for the two V notches that will take the string. Cut the notches through the cover and all the pages.
Tie the string with a double knot and bow, or use an elastic band to keep all the pages together. Pages may be easily removed and extra pages added by undoing the string.

Evaluation: Were the children able to follow your directions?
Was the folding, cutting and tying done carefully?
Were the children pleased with the results?

Activity: Fish collage

Concept: Colour/shape/pattern.

Aim: To make the children aware of
                    the main features of fish.
                    To consolidate previous work
                    on colour, shape and pattern.

Resources needed: Pictures and slides of colourful fish. Projector and screen.
                        Any cheap paper; colourful offcuts of paper and material; paste; scissors; pencils.

Preparation: Set up projector. Cut paper to a variety of sizes. Give out paper and pencils.

Introduction: Show the slides of tropical fish, pointing out the fish's main features: tail, fins, eyes, mouth, pattern, scales, colour.
                        Discuss pictures of fish in books and ask some children to describe them in terms of the above features. Ask the children to make a collage picture of a fish that they have seen, or to invent one that no one else has seen.

Development: Suggest that the children should draw the outline of their fish first, then fill in the shape with pieces of cut or torn paper. Tell the children to decide whether their fish has a repeat pattern or haphazard colour markings before sticking down their pieces of paper.
                        When finished, the fish might be cut out and mounted against a contrasting background, or the children might prefer to add weeds, rocks, etc. to their picture.

Evaluation: Were the children able to remember the main features of a fish?
                        Were materials handled properly?
                        Were there any unusual results?

Activity:	Wave collages.
Concept:	Rhythm.
Aim:	To express the movement of waves.

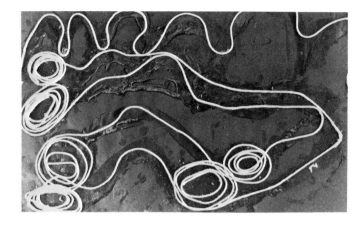

Resources needed:	1. Any sort of background paper; paper offcuts; string or wool; paste; scissors. 2. Pictures of the sea; photographs and artists' impressions. 3. Record of wave noises; sea poems.
Preparation:	Give out materials.
Introduction:	Read the sea poems and listen to the record of wave sounds. Refer to the rhythm of the waves. Show the pictures and discuss the patterns made by the waves, using words like swirling, rippling, crashing, rushing, etc. Demonstrate with a piece of string how the motion of waves might be suggested.
Development:	Invite the children to use string, wool or cut paper stuck on to their background sheet, in order to express the movement of the waves. Play the record again while the children are working and encourage them to make wave noises at the same time.
Evaluation:	Did the final results suggest the movement of waves?

Activity: Fish – press printing.

Concept: Pattern.

Aim: To consolidate previous work on repeat patterns.
To allow practice at simple block printing.

Resources needed:
1. Newspaper; any cheap, white paper; corks and other small printing blocks; small pieces of foam rubber that fit into jam jar lids; dark, creamy paint; pencil.
2. A real fish or a stuffed fish.

Preparation: Display the results of Session 45.
Cover desks with newspaper.
Give each child a foam pad with a small block of paint, and a cork.

Introduction: Discuss the results of Session 45.
Show children the fish and talk about its scales. Point out that they repeat the same shape over and over again, which we call a pattern. Refer to previous work on repeat patterns – Session 45.
Demonstrate how to make prints from a cork. Put about a teaspoonful of creamy paint on to a foam pad. Dab it with a cork and press it on to a sheet of paper. Show how a repeat pattern is formed. Ask the children to either print a picture of the fish in the classroom, or they could invent their own shape.

Development: Tell the children to draw the outline of the fish so that its nose touches one end of the paper and its tail touches the other. Proceed with printing the pattern of the scales as shown until the fish is covered. Fins, gills, etc. could be printed with the end of a ruler.
Children could complete their pictures by adding seaweed, pebbles, etc., or the fish could be cut out and mounted on to a class frieze.

Evaluation: Did the results indicate an understanding of repeat patterns?
Were the children handling the materials properly?

Activity:	Underwater picture with chalk.
Concept:	Colour/shape.
Aim:	To encourage the use of appropriate colours. To introduce chalk techniques.

Resources needed:
1. Newspaper; sugar paper; coloured chalks; paste; scissors; offcuts of paper suitable for seaweed, rocks, etc.
2. Pictures of life under the sea.
3. Any poems connected with life under the sea, e.g. 'The Dead Crab' by Andrew Young, 'The Whale' by Hilaire Belloc.

Preparation: Cut paper to approximately 40 × 30 cm. Cover tables with newspaper and give out materials. Display the results of Session 47.

Introduction: Briefly refer to the results of Session 47. Read the poems and discuss the undersea pictures, paying particular attention to the colour found in the water and the types and shapes of seaweed. Ask the children to imagine that they were sitting on the sea bed. What would they notice.
Demonstrate how to merge the chalks with the fingers in order to soften the colours.

Development: Invite the children to cover their paper in chalk, merging with their fingers in order to create a feeling of water. They may then add any other details by sticking cut or torn paper shapes to this background.

Evaluation: Did the children merge the appropriate colours?
Were they able to express the feeling of being underwater?

Activity:	Undersea monsters – paintings.
Concept:	Colour/texture/pattern.
Aim:	To stimulate imaginative responses. To encourage the expressive use of colour.

Resources needed:
1. Newspaper; any cheap paper; water jars, one between two; paint rags, one each; primary colours and black and white; brushes; palettes.
2. Pictures of prehistoric creatures and strangely exotic underwater creatures.

Preparation:
Cut paper to a variety of sizes.
Cover tables with newspaper.
Give out materials.

Introduction:
Tell the children about the Loch Ness monster and of any other strange creatures that live on the ocean bed that no-one has ever seen. Ask if the children could imagine what they might look like. Invite suggestions.
Show some of the pictures and discuss features not normally found on animals we know.
Invite them to invent their own monster that no-one has ever seen, and to paint it without any preliminary drawing.

Development:
While work is in progress, children should be encouraged to consider details such as whether it has a pattern, fins, textured skin, toes or flippers, etc.
Finally, ask the children to put in the water, seaweed, rocks, etc. This could be done with paint, chalk or pieces of paper stuck on.

Evaluation:
Were the results imaginative?
Did the children handle the paint skilfully?
Were there any unexpected outcomes?

Activity: Easter bonnet parade.

Concept: Shape/colour/pattern.

Aim: To encourage selection and discrimination.
To encourage observation of features.

Resources needed:
1. Sugar paper; tissue paper; feathers; patterned wallpaper samples; water jars; paint rags; paints; brushes; palettes; scissors; PVA adhesive and spatulas.
2. Pictures of fancy hats or bonnets of different shapes. Try to get photographs of an Easter bonnet parade or Royal Ascot.

Preparation: Cut paper to approximately 20 × 30 cm.
Cover tables with newspaper.
Give out painting materials and paper.

Introduction: Show children the pictures of hats and discuss the parades. Invite them to paint a picture of a woman attending an Easter bonnet parade. Tell them to make the hat very large and important in their picture. Try to imagine what the woman is thinking about and show this by the way that you paint her face. Is she happy and smiling, miserable or surprised? Tell the children to study the expression on their friends faces and to pull faces in the mirror if necessary.

Development: The children may wish to paint their bonnet on a separate piece of paper, then cut it out and stick it on to their painting of the lady. They may then decorate the bonnet with feathers, little pieces of tissue paper screwed up to suggest flowers, or parts of patterns cut from wallpaper.
Discussions might centre on the choice of colours and whether the woman's dress matches her hat, etc.

Evaluation: Did the faces have a particular expression?
Was there discussion about the colours and patterns?
Did the finished pictures indicate that some thought had gone into the choice of colours and patterns?

Activity:	The colour wheel.
Concept:	Colour.
Aim:	To introduce the primary colours and to demonstrate how we arrive at the secondary colours.

Resources needed: Newspapers; any white paper; water jars, one between two; paint rags, one each; paints, red, yellow, blue (see colour notes on page 145); brushes; palettes; circular objects for drawing circles, approximately 15 cm in diameter; pencils; rulers.

Preparation: Cut paper to approximately 20 × 30 cm. Cover tables with newspaper. Give out materials. Draw a circle on the board and divide it into six equal parts.

Introduction: Instruct the children how to draw a circle on their paper and divide it up, as you did, into six roughly equal parts. Tell them to write the word *blue* very lightly in one of the segments; then to miss a segment and write *red* very lightly in the next; miss a segment and write *yellow* in the next. Explain that these are known as the primary colours. They cannot be made up by mixing other colours together. However, when we mix the primary colours together we can get lots of other colours.

Development: Ask the children to mix enough creamy blue paint to fill the blue segment, then to paint it in carefully. Wash and dry the brush and do the same with the red and yellow. Mix equal portions of yellow and red in the palette, and fill in the blank segment between yellow and red with the resultant orange. Now mix yellow and blue to make green and fill the appropriate segment and finally blue and red to make violet. Orange, green and violet are known as the secondary colours. If there is time, ask the children to see what happens when they mix equal quantities of yellow, red and blue. They should arrive at brown.

Evaluation: Were the children able to mix the appropriate colours?
Did they handle the paint properly?

Activity:	Painting brightly-coloured birds.
Concept:	Colour.
Aim:	To use the skills learned in Session 51. To encourage observation of natural colour and to practise mixing it.

Resources needed:
1. Newspaper; any white paper; water jars, one between two; paint rags, one each; paints, primary colours plus black and white; range of brushes; palettes.
2. Slides and pictures of brightly-coloured birds – parrots, budgies, etc., live birds if possible or a stuffed one from a museum.

Preparation: Cut paper to approximately 20 × 30 cm. Cover tables with newspaper and give out materials. Display the results of the previous Session.

Introduction: Show children the birds and discuss their colouring as fully as possible. Refer to the primary and secondary colours on their colour circles. Draw up a list of colours noted.

Development: Ask the children to paint a picture of any one of the birds, mixing the colours where necessary. It is not necessary to draw the bird first, though it might be helpful to decide on its general overall colour, and to paint in the whole of the bird in a thin wash of this colour to start with. Discussion will arise about how to mix colours other than those mixed in the previous session, and children should be encouraged to experiment with different combinations, e.g. yellow and black will give a different green to yellow and blue. Brown can also be made by adding a little black to red.

Evaluation: Did children mix the secondary colours easily? Did the paintings indicate that the children had observed the natural colours of the birds?

Activity: Printing from feathers.

Concept: Colour/texture.

Aim: To consolidate work of the
previous two Sessions.
To introduce transfer printing.

Resources needed:
1. Newspaper; any white paper; water jars, one between two; paint rags, one each; paints, ready-mixed in jars – red, yellow, blue, orange, green, violet; brushes.
2. Feathers.

Preparation:
Display work from previous Session.
Ask children to bring in feathers.
Cut the white paper to approximately 5 × 15 cm – ten pieces to each child.
Cut some newspaper to approximately 10 × 20 cm – twenty pieces to each child.
Mix paint to a creamy consistency.
Cover tables with newspaper.
Prepare somewhere for the prints to dry.

Introduction:
Refer to the work on display and have a quick recap on primary and secondary colours. Demonstrate how to make a print of a feather. Place the feather on a small piece of newspaper. Hold it steady with one hand and paint it with the other. Brush off surplus paint so that the feather has an even layer of paint. Place the feather, painted side down, on to a small piece of white paper. Put another small piece of newspaper on top and rub gently all over, trying not to move the feather. Straightaway throw both pieces of painted newspaper into the bin. Remove the feather carefully and put the print somewhere to dry. The ribbed texture of the feather should be apparent, but this will depend on the evenness of the paint.

Development:
Ask the children to make about ten prints ready for their bird mask. They should use either warm colours (yellows, oranges, reds) or cold colours (blues, greens, violets).

Evaluation:
Could the children recall which were the primary and secondary colours?
Could the texture of the feather be seen on the prints?

Activity: Bird mask.

Concept: Colour/pattern/form.

Aim: To consolidate previous work
on colour and pattern.
To introduce the idea of a
symmetrical design.
To demonstrate simple paper
sculpture technique.

Resources needed:
1. Scissors; PVA adhesive; spatulas; stapler; thin card; rulers; pencils.
2. Feather prints made during previous Session.

Preparation: Cut card to approximately 20 × 30 cm and 20 × 15 cm.

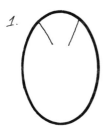   

Introduction: Demonstrate how to make the base of the mask in the four stages illustrated above.
Cut the larger piece of card to an oval shape and make two slits at the top.
Fold over the flaps and staple or stick them. Put the mask on and mark the position of the eyes.
Make similar flaps at the bottom and stick down.
Cut the smaller card to a beak shape and stick it to the base with two small flaps.

Development: When the children have completed their base, ask them to cut out their feather prints and stick them to the base. Tell them to overlap the feathers slightly and try to achieve a pattern that is the same on both sides of the mask. This is known as a symmetrical design. The children might wish to base their ideas on a bird that they have seen, or they could invent their own designs.

Evaluation: Could the children construct the base, using the cutting and folding technique?
Were the patterns symmetrical and bird-like in appearance?

67

Activity: Painting imaginary birds.

Concept: Colour/pattern/texture.

Aim: To stimulate an imaginative response.

Resources needed:
1. Crayons, felt-tip pens; newspaper; any white paper; water jars; paint rags; paints, primary colours plus black and white; brushes.
2. Slides and pictures of colourful and unusual birds, including any that are extinct.
3. Recording of bird songs.

Preparation: Display the bird masks from Session 54. Cover the tables with newspaper. Cut paper to various sizes and give out the materials.

Introduction: Show the slides and pictures of the birds and listen to the recordings of bird calls. Discuss the colours, and point out any unusual features.
Tell the children of birds that no longer exist because they are extinct, and, if possible, show pictures of some.
Invite the children to draw or paint a picture of a bird that they think might have existed, but no-one knows about it. Ask them to think carefully about the colours and unusual markings or feathers that the bird might have had.

Development: The first attempt might be stilted, and children should be allowed time to develop this idea. They might, therefore, be asked to draw or paint more than one bird. If the children decide to paint, preliminary drawing is unnecessary.
Time might be allowed at the end for a brief discussion about the work. Children might like to invent names and take it in turns to make the noise that their bird would have made.

Evaluation: Did the children respond imaginatively?
Were there any unusual results?

Activity:	Painting owls.
Concept:	Colour/texture/pattern.
Aim:	To consolidate previous work on mixing tints and shades. To increase the children's awareness of colour.

Resources needed:

1. Newspaper; different coloured and white paper; water jars, one between two; paint rags, one each; primary colours plus black and white; range of brushes; palettes.
2. Preferably a live bird or a stuffed bird from the museum. Choose one that is basically tints and shades of one hue. If it is impossible to find a real bird, then slides and photographs would do, but these are a poor substitute for the real thing – even if it is dead!

Preparation: Cut paper to a variety of sizes. Cover tables with newspaper and give out materials.

Introduction: Show the bird(s) to the children. Ask if the bird is basically one colour. Is it only that colour or are there other colours. How many tints and shades of the main hue are there? Do they know how to mix the main hue? Can they remember two ways of mixing brown? (Sessions 51 and 52).
How is a tint made? How is a shade made? (Session 36).

Development: Ask the children to mix the basic hue of one of the birds. They should then mix in their palette at least five more tints and shades of that hue before they start painting. Choose the lightest to paint in the main shape of the bird, then fill in as much detail of pattern as possible. Remind the children about washing out their brush and changing their water when it becomes muddy.

Evaluation: Did the results indicate that the children had closely observed the colours of the bird? Were the children able to recognise and mix the different tints and shades?

Activity: Owl collage.

Concept: Colour/texture/pattern.

Aim: To consolidate previous experience of choosing colours.
To increase children's awareness of colour and texture.

See Colour Plate C

Resources needed:
1. Newspaper; paste; brushes; scissors; pencils or chalk; range of paper offcuts in appropriate colours; coloured magazines; old wallpaper books; sugar paper for a base, preferably in a colour that will contrast with the collage material.
2. Preferably the same live or stuffed birds used in the previous session. If that is impossible, then slides and photographs would do, but as before these are a poor substitute for the real thing.

Preparation: Display the paintings produced during the previous Session. Sort out paper offcuts according to their colour. Cover tables with newspaper. Cut the sugar paper to approximately 30 × 40 cm. Give out paste, brushes and scissors.

Introduction: Discuss the birds and pictures of birds used during the previous Session. Invite the children to choose either the same bird or a different one, and to represent it with collage materials. A simple outline in chalk or pencil may be used as a starting point, then pieces of paper should be cut or torn up to represent feathers. These should be pasted down so that they slightly overlap one another, just as real feathers do.

Development: Keep referring back to what the children have learned about colour, and encourage them to choose appropriate colours. Discuss the texture of the feathers, and ways of achieving that feeling of light fluffiness. Are there any designs in the wallpaper that might be useful – ferns, leaves, feathers, etc.

Evaluation: Did the children choose appropriate colours for their bird?
Did some results convey the texture of a bird's feathers better than others, and why?

Activity: Collage of imaginary birds.

Concept: Colour/shape/texture.

Aim: To stimulate an imaginative
response.
To use existing patterns and
textures inventively.

See Colour Plate S

**Resources
needed:**   Wallpaper sample books; paste; scissors; sugar paper.

Preparation: Display the results of the previous three Sessions. Cut sugar paper to approximately
20 × 30 cm. Distribute other materials.

Introduction: Discuss the results of the previous three Sessions. With reference to Session 57, ask which
ones successfully conveyed the texture of a bird's feathers, and why. Ask the children to
imagine birds that did not have feathers all over, and to use parts of wallpaper designs to show
what they looked like. They can be strange and unusual, or they could be similar to a bird
already in existence, but with different pieces added.

Development: Children sort through the wallpaper samples, cutting out any pieces that might come in
useful. The pieces should not be stuck down immediately, but moved about on the paper until
a satisfactory arrangement is arrived at. Ask the children to consider whether or not their bird
is mainly one colour, whether it can fly or swim, has a long neck or legs, is beautiful or funny
to look at, etc.

Evaluation: Were the results imaginative?
Were patterns and textures used inventively?

Activity: Animal collage.

Concept: Shape/texture.

Aim: To encourage observation of natural texture and to express it through the medium of collage.

See Colour Plate J

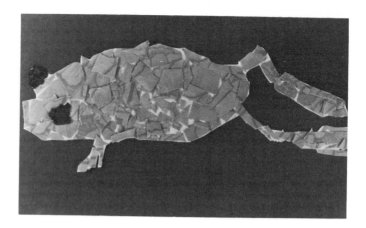

Resources needed:
1. Different collage materials that might convey the texture of the animals in question; PVA adhesive; spatulas; cereal boxes for bases; chalk.
2. Live or stuffed animals that have interesting textures to their surface, e.g. tortoise, hedgehog. If that is impossible, then slides and photographs would do, but these are a poor substitute for the real thing – even if it is dead.

Preparation: Display the animals and/or pictures of animals. Ask the children to provide a cereal box and any suitable collage materials for the animals. Cut the boxes into sheets of card. Sort the collage materials into groups and, if possible, have a separate container for each.

Introduction: Refer to the animals on display and discuss their texture. Let the children touch them, if possible, and describe what it feels like. Ask if they have felt anything quite like it.
Is there anything amongst the range of collage materials that might give the same feel if it were stuck on to a backing?

Development: Ask the children to carefully consider the *shape* of the animal and to draw a simple outline with chalk on the plain side of their cardboard.
Study all the collage materials and decide which ones would be most useful to make the same texture as the real animal. Do not worry if the colour is not right, as it is the *texture* that we are concerned with. Arrange some of the materials first before sticking them down.
Tell the children to test their collage by closing their eyes and running their fingers over it.

Evaluation: Did the results indicate that the children had carefully observed the texture of the animals?
Did the children choose appropriate materials?
Did they manage to get the shape of their animal in proportion?

Activity: Clay work.

Concept: Form/texture.

Aim: To provide the opportunity to explore the expressive qualities of clay.

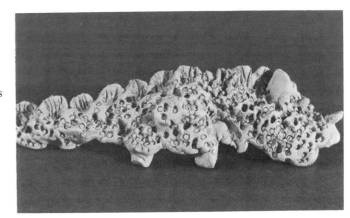

Resources needed:
1. Clay; newspaper; damp cloth or plastic bag; lolly sticks, sharpened twigs, etc., that will serve as modelling tools.
2. Pictures of prehistoric animals that do *not* have long, thin limbs or bodies, and are preferably textured or patterned.

Preparation: Cover tables with newspaper.
Prepare clay so that each child has a ball about the size of a small orange.
Keep the clay covered with a damp rag or in a plastic bag, until it is needed as it very quickly dries out.

Introduction: Show children the pictures and discuss the creatures' form. Point out any unusual features and refer to details of texture, pattern, and so on. Ask the children to make a prehistoric animal with clay. This could be similar to one that they have seen in the pictures, or they could invent one of their own.
Tell them that they should keep the clay in one piece and should roll or pinch the clay to make the basic shape of their creature. Finally, any markings or texture may be added with the modelling tools.

Development: Clay should be allowed to dry slowly and may take a week to dry thoroughly. Dry clay is extremely brittle and should be handled with utmost care. For this reason it is not advisable for young children to decorate their models. If firing is out of the question (see Session 120) they can be strengthened by dipping or coating thoroughly in PVA. Teachers might feel inclined, however, to treat these exploratory efforts as being ephemeral and after a period on display, they could be reduced back to clay to be re-used (see page 158).

Evaluation: Were the children able to make the basic form of their creatures?
Were there any imaginative responses?

Stages 3 and 4 – lower juniors

Each stage comprises fifteen Sessions, allowing for about five Sessions each term. Each Session aims to either introduce or increase awareness of an artistic concept or concepts which are stated at the beginning of each Session outline. Hopefully, teachers will augment these Sessions with others that will further increase awareness of these concepts, and also allow children time to develop newly-acquired skills.

Children of around this age are becoming more and more fascinated by reality, and so it is important to work from first-hand experience wherever possible. Although storage space is a constant headache in schools, children should be encouraged to make collections of things that are visually exciting and teachers should develop the child's artistic language by discussing the collections in terms of shape, texture, colour, pattern, tone and form.

Imaginative work can be developed from observation of real objects, natural and man-made, stories, poetry, pictures and music.

Stage 3

Stage 4

Activity: Silhouettes.

Concept: Shape.

Aim: To increase the children's powers of observation. To make them more aware of the shape of objects.

Resources needed:
1. Any white paper; black paper; black felt-tip pens; scissors; pencils.
2. About ten objects that would be instantly recognised in silhouette; cardboard box to take the objects.
3. A translucent screen, made by pinning tracing paper or tissue paper to an old picture frame.

Preparation: Cut white paper to approximately 20 × 30 cm.

Introduction: Tell the class that you are starting with a guessing game. Take the box of objects to a window and display them one at a time behind the translucent screen so that the children only see the object in silhouette. If a suitable window is not available, use a table lamp as the source of light. Children might write down their answers and check how many were correct.
Next, show objects behind the screen that have interesting or distinctive features. Turn them round slowly so that at times they are unrecognisable. Discuss which shapes make them easily recognisable.

Development: Ask children to choose objects from the box, or any others in the room that would be recognisable in silhouette. Tell them to hold their object behind the screen and turn it until they have decided which view they will draw in silhouette with a black felt-tip pen on white paper, or to cut it from black paper after lightly drawing it in pencil.

Evaluation: Did most of the children succeed at the guessing game?
Did their silhouette pictures indicate that they were observing shapes?
Were most of the objects recognisable?

A   A drawing and rubbings transferred on to a T-shirt. Session 114.

B   A copy of a painting by Gainsborough. Session 116.

C   A collage from wallpaper, as a result of seeing a real owl. Session 57.

D   Starry Night by Van Gogh. Session 117.

E   Silhouette compositions. Session 101.

F   Painting. Session 15.

G   Learning how to use colour. Session 36.

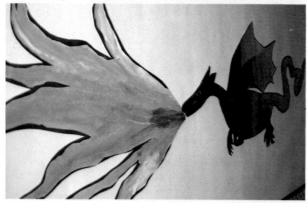

H   Mixing tints and shades of one colour. Session 69.

I   Using colour to express a mood or emotion. Session 70.

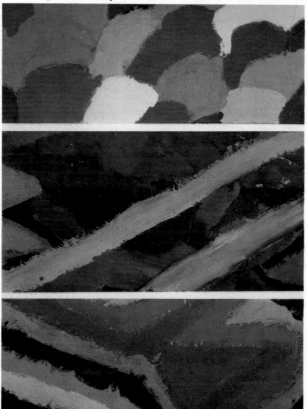

J   A tortoise. Session 59.

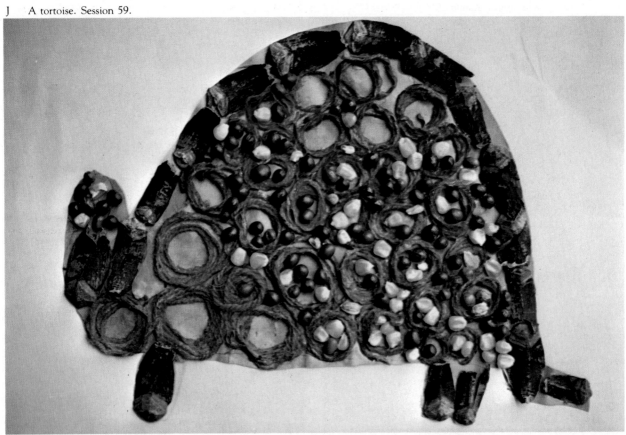

K   Learning about the primary colours. Session 13.

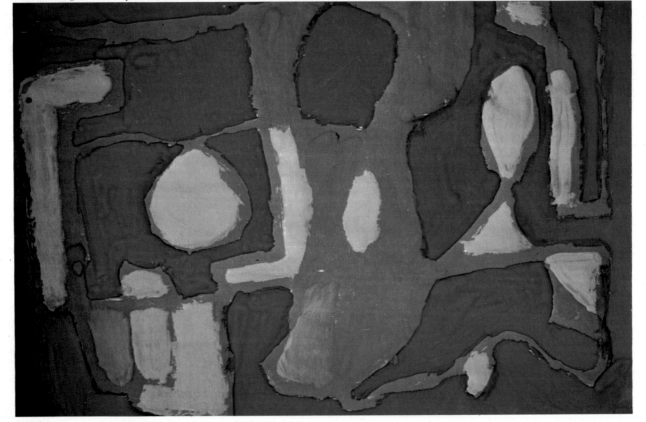

L   A bonfire party. Session 63.

M   A Christmas frieze. Session 80.

N   Fireworks. Session 39.

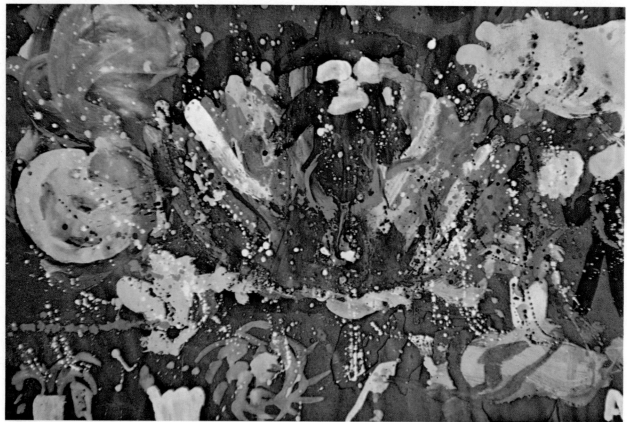

O   Imaginary city. An extension of Sessions 108 and 109.

P   A fabric collage and embroidery inspired by an altar cloth seen in
     Worcester Cathedral. An extension of Session 107.

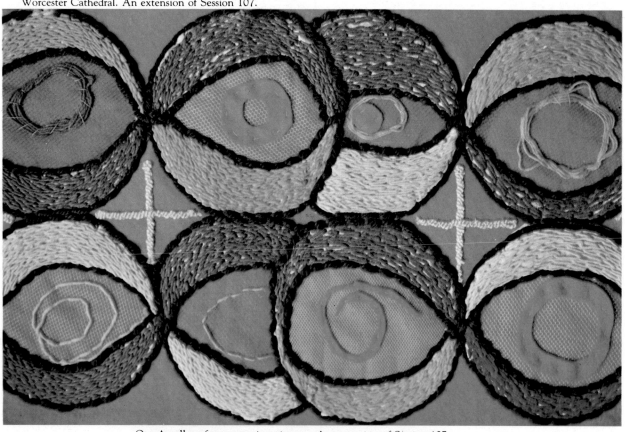

Q   A collage from magazine pictures. An extension of Session 107.

R   Learning about yellow. An extension of Session 35.

S   An imaginary bird. An extension of Session 58.

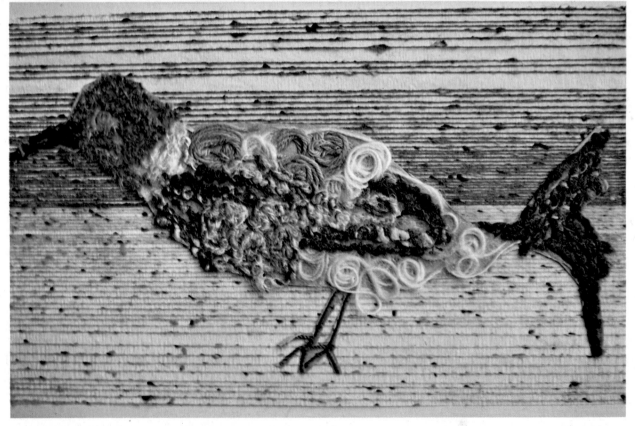

Activity: Halloween silhouettes.

Concept: Shape.

Aim: To consolidate work of the
                 previous Session.
                 To stimulate an imaginative
                 response.

Resources   1. Any white paper; black paper; black felt-tip pens; scissors; pencils.
needed: 2. Photographs of witches; objects or photographs of items usually associated with Halloween
                    – broomstick, cat, bottles, etc.
                 3. Poems or stories about witches and Halloween, e.g. 'The Witch', 'I Saw Three Witches'
                 by Walter de la Mare, 'Three Poor Witches' by Edith Sitwell.

Preparation: Display the results of Session 61.
                 Cut white paper to approximately 20 × 30 cm.

Introduction: Discuss the results of Session 61, and praise the efforts of those who managed to produce
                 recognisable silhouette shapes.
                 Read the poems and stories connected with Halloween.
                 Ask the children for a list of items suitable for a silhouette Halloween picture. Ask which
                 characteristics of a witch they would choose to emphasise, and what the witch might be doing
                 in their picture.

Development: Ask the children to make a silhouette Halloween picture by drawing with black felt-tip pens
                 on white paper, or cutting from black paper, or a combination of both methods.
                 Although the teacher's photographs and resource items might be used as reference, it should
                 be stressed that it is not essential that these items should *necessarily* appear in the picture.
                 They should be used merely to stimulate the children's imagination.

Evaluation: Were the children able to make pictures entirely in silhouette?
                 Were there any unusual or very imaginative results?

Activity: Firework party.

Concept: Colour/shape.

Aim: To consolidate previous work on silhouettes.
To encourage expression of an experience.

See Colour Plate L

Resources needed:

1. Black paper; scissors; pencils; offcuts of paper, tissue and Cellophane in any warm or fiery colours; paste; tracing paper approximately 50 × 60 cm (if the picture is to be mounted on the window), or any white paper approximately 50 × 60 cm.
2. Slides or pictures of bonfires or buildings ablaze, with figures in silhouette.
Poems or stories about bonfire night.

Preparation: Display results of the previous Session. Cut black paper into pieces approximately 20 × 10 cm.

Introduction: Read the poems or stories and ask some of the children to describe their own experience of bonfire night. Ask how big the bonfire was in relation to the height of the people. Did the children notice any silhouettes against the fire or the sky?
Show the slides or pictures of figures silhouetted against fire.
Invite the children to make a picture of a bonfire party, using coloured paper to describe the bonfire and black paper to describe anything else.

Development: Children may work individually or in groups. Suggest that the bonfire should be put in first, and that this should almost fill the backing sheet. Children should then be able to decide on the height of the figures. Ask them to think about what the people were doing at the bonfire and how this would be described in silhouette.
If children are working on a tracing-paper backing for a window-mounted picture, then tissue and Cellophane paper would probably be more effective for the flames.

Evaluation: Did the results convey the excitement and drama of bonfire night?
Were the silhouette figures recognisable?

Activity:	Christmas decorations.
Concept:	Pattern/line/shape.
Aim:	To consolidate children's knowledge of radial designs. To increase children's manipulative skills.

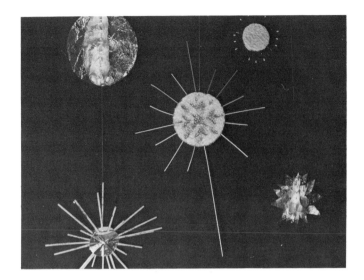

Resources needed:
1. Polystyrene offcuts; drinking straws; matchsticks; cocktail sticks; aluminium foil; large needles and cotton; sharp cutters; knitting needles.
2. Many different pictures of radiating, circular designs – stylised suns, stars, flowers, etc.

Preparation: Ask the children to bring in pictures of radiating designs, and display these with your own. Ask the children to collect silver paper bigger than 10 × 10 cm; clean matchsticks and cocktail sticks.

Introduction: Refer to the pictures of radiating designs and see how many are symmetrical. Explain how symmetry comes about in a round, radiating design.
Ask the children why they think the star is an important symbol at Christmas time.
Suggest that they make many different types of stars for decorative purposes using the materials provided, and any more they can think of.
All the stars should have a circular design that radiates symmetrically.

Development: *Group A.* The children start by cutting circles from polystyrene. Holes are made with knitting needles for the drinking straws and matchsticks. Finished stars are suspended by cotton.
Group B. Cut four identical circles 10 × 10 cm or larger, from kitchen foil or silver paper. Put them together then fold in half to make a crease. Open them out and sew all four together, using a running stitch, along the crease. Open out part way to make a three-dimensional star. If you prefer, cut round the edges before opening out.
These stars should blend with decorations suggested in Sessions 79, 110, 111.

Evaluation: Did the children make symmetrical radiating designs?
Did the children add their own ideas and materials to yours?
Did they handle the materials skilfully?

Activity: The Three Kings.

Concept: Colour/shape.

Aim: To encourage the choice of
                  colours which harmonise.
                  To encourage discrimination
                  in choosing collage materials.

Resources   1. Any cheap paper for backing; paste; brushes; scissors; chalk; a variety of paper and fabric
needed: offcuts, sorted according to colours and preferably in boxes; collage material for hair,
                      beards, etc.
                   2. Photographs from colour magazines of people wearing interesting colour combinations.

Preparation: Cut paper to approximately 40 × 30 cm. Give out scissors, chalk and paste.

Introduction: Tell the children the Christmas story. Ask the children to imagine what the Three Kings
                   looked like? Could they describe their clothing, what they were carrying, their hair style, etc.
                   Ask questions about choosing colours for clothes, which colours look nice together and why.
                   Show photographs of people wearing interesting colour combinations, and discuss the effect
                   of the colours – frivolous, daring, sombre, stately, etc.
                   Suggest that they draw the general outline of one of the kings in chalk, but not to worry about
                   details.

Development: Tell the children to consider carefully which collage materials would best convey the type of
                   clothing worn by a very rich king of an eastern country. Suggest putting materials together
                   first to see if they match before cutting them out or sticking them down. Encourage them to
                   choose colours which harmonise. If they are unsure how to do this, refer to the colour circle
                   and suggest choosing colours from the same 'family', e.g. browns or greens. Finally, add
                   details or accesories to indicate wealth or importance.

Evaluation: Were the children fairly discriminating in their choice of colour.
                   Did they tend to choose colours that harmonised or was the final effect jumpy?

Activity: Green display.

Concept: Colour/tone.

Aim: To make the children aware of the different greens that exist in their environment.
To consolidate previous work done on tone.

Resources needed:
1. As many different green backing materials as you can find: paper, Cellophane, fabrics, etc.
2. Any green objects that you can find. Reproductions of paintings or magazine photographs where green is the predominant colour.
3. As many different plain green papers or material as you can find, cut to the same size: about 15 × 20 cm.

Preparation: Prepare a table with display board behind, preferably in the classroom. Cover all surfaces with green paper or material, ready for the children's offerings. Tell the children to bring in things from home that are entirely green and to put them on the table. Display the pictures.

Introduction: Ask the children to talk about the things brought in and ask questions aimed at increasing their understanding of green. Which is the lightest green on display? Are there others exactly the same shade of green? How many different greens are there? Which is the darkest green? Could you give the green names e.g. light green, dark green, blue green, pea green, grass green, etc.?

Development: Using some of the words previously mentioned as a start the children write labels to describe the colour of six objects or backing sheets of their choice. When all the labels are in position, discuss the names given to the colours. If some objects have more than one label, get a class opinion as to which one is the most appropriate and remove any extras. Using these names as a guide, ask the children to name the sheets of coloured paper that you prepared. Ask which is the lightest and darkest and place these two at opposite ends of a table. In turn, ask children to place the other sheets in a tonal scale going from light to dark.
Ask for suggestions as to how we might categorise all the greens, and then place objects in families, e.g. yellow greens, blue greens, etc.

Evaluation: Was there much interest in the display?
Did the introduction generate discussion?
Did the children recall previous work done on tone?

Activity: Designing a folder cover.

Concept: Shape/pattern/colour.

Aim: To introduce children to the
notion of repeat patterns.
To consolidate previous work
on green.

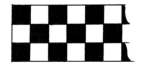 or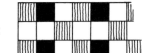

**Resources
needed:**   Each child will need: black paper; two different shades of plain green paper or material; glue;
scissors; ruler and pencil.
Teacher will need: examples of simple repeat patterns made into designs, e.g. wallpaper; spare
sheets of green paper.

Preparation: Cut black paper to approximately 40 × 30 cm. Previous to this Session tell the children to
collect two sheets of plain paper or material, which should be quite different shades of green.
Each should be approximately 20 × 30 cm.

Introduction: Show examples of repeat patterns and explain the basic principle of repeat designs. Explain
that the children will design a folder cover using only *squares* that must touch one another, in
two different shades of green. Demonstrate on the board one or two ways of achieving this.
See illustration above left.
Some shapes should touch the top of the paper.
When you are sure that everyone understands the principle of repeat patterns, rub the
example from the board and tell the class that you want them to invent their own patterns.

Development: The children should start by folding their black paper in half to form the cover of the folder.
Then they should cut ten squares from each of their pieces of paper or material. These should
be 2–3 cm square and fit exactly into the width of the folder cover. e.g. if the folder is 20 cm
wide, the squares should be exactly 2 cm square.
Tell the children to start right at the top of their paper and place the squares in a repeat
pattern that goes right across the paper. Time should be spent experimenting before the
design is finally stuck into position. More squares can be cut up as they are needed. Try to
allow time to discuss results. Ask the children to describe their work accurately using a
suitable name for the greens used.

Evaluation: Did the children bring paper or material that was different tonally?
Were they able to make designs that repeated?
Did their discussion indicate that they had remembered how to categorise greens?

Activity: Collage in green.

Concept: Colour.

Aim: To make children more aware of the colour green.

Resources needed: Each child will need: any sort of backing paper; at least one magazine with plenty of coloured pictures; green offcuts of paper and fabric; scissors; chalk; glue.
Teacher will need: photographs of unusual flora and fauna.

Preparation: Cut paper to approximately 20 × 30 cm.
Hand out all materials except the magazines which tend to distract the children's attention.

Introduction: Tell a story of a fantastic space flight to the Green Planet where *everything* is different shades of green. No-one has ever been there and the class are asked to imagine what might be there, e.g. inhabitants, flora, fauna, etc. Having decided what it is they wish to represent, the children are asked to make a quick outline with chalk but it should be stressed that any detail at this stage is a complete waste of time. The drawing should completely fill the paper touching all four sides of the paper in places. Show children photographs of very unusual plants and animals which might stimulate imaginative ideas, but stress that they must not copy them.

Development: The children search the magazines for areas of green which they tear or cut out and use for their collage. It is best not to stick down pieces immediately, but to wait until most of the outline is filled before doing so. Encourage the children to be inventive and original, by reminding them that the creatures and plants on this planet will be quite unlike anything seen on earth.
Results might be cut out and mounted together on a frieze of the Green Planet.

Evaluation: Were there any original results?
Did the children enjoy this Session?
What did the discussion reveal?

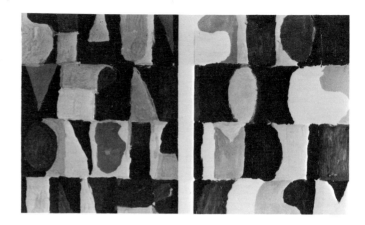

Activity: Name painting.

Concept: Colour.

Aim: To consolidate previous work done on tints and shades.

See Colour Plate H

Resources needed: Newspaper; any white paper; coloured chalk; water jars, one between two; paint rags, one each; red, yellow, blue, black and white paint for each group; brushes.

Preparation: Cover desks with newspaper and give out materials.
Cut paper to approximately 30 × 40 cm.

Introduction: Remind the children that a tint is made by adding white to a hue and a shade is made by adding black to a hue. Tell the children to fold their paper in half, then in half again, thus dividing it into four equal strips across the paper. Flatten the paper out with the creases going horizontally. Each child writes his own name in chalk on the first strip, so that each letter touches the top of the paper and the first crease. Use capitals only and spread the letters out so that there is space between them. If the name will not fit on the first strip go on to the next strip. Keep repeating the name until the sheet is entirely filled with letters. Demonstrate this on the board. Point out that the page is now divided into lots of different shapes.

Development: Ask the children to choose a primary colour (yellow, red, blue) or a secondary colour (orange, green, purple) and fill about six shapes with that hue. Children then make tints and shades of the hue and fill in all the other shapes, covering up the chalk lines, too. When mixing their paint, the children should be advised to make thick, creamy paint and enough to paint two or three shapes. Point out that if the tone of two adjacent shapes is too close, they will not stand out against one another. When the paintings are finished it might be difficult to read the names, but this is unimportant.
Discuss the finished results.

Evaluation: Did the children remember the names of the primary and secondary colours?
Did they handle their paint skilfully?
What did the discussion reveal?

Activity:	Expressing moods.
Concept:	Colour.
Aim:	To teach that colour has emotive value.

See Colour Plate I

Resources needed:
1. Newspaper; any white paper; range of coloured paper; water jars, one between two; paint rags, one each; full range of paints for each group; brushes.
2. Reproductions of Picasso's blue period and any pictures with bright, cheerful colours. A colour circle (Session 51).

Preparation:
Display paintings done during Session 69.
Cover desks with newspaper and give out materials.
Cut paper to approximately 40 × 30 cm.

Introduction:
Refer to the paintings done in Session 69 and ask which ones seem to have happy or sad colours and why. Which paintings could be described as 'angry', 'warm', 'restful'. Ask the children for other words evoked by the colours.
Show your example of bright, cheerful pictures and discuss how the colours affect the mood of the picture.
Ask one of the children to hold one of the Picasso reproductions so that the rest of the class cannot see it and then to describe it as fully as possible, so that the other children can imagine it. Particular attention should be paid to the colours that the artist has used.
Show and discuss the other Picasso's and invite suggestions as to how certain colours would have been mixed. Ask the children if any one colour predominates in these paintings. Besides many different blues, ask which other colours he used in these pictures and show their position on the colour circle, relative to blue. It will be noticed that most of the colours are grouped near to blue in the colour circle.

Development:
Invite the children to do an abstract painting based on one of the following words: fear, joy, peace, love, hate, vigorous, lively, jealous, gloomy, etc. Stress that recognisable objects are not necessary. The mood of the picture should be expressed mainly through colour, though simple shapes may also be used. Paintings should be started directly with a brush, with no preliminary drawing. The paper should be covered entirely with paint.
Discuss some of the results.

Evaluation:
Did the paintings evoke ideas or emotions?
Did the results provoke discussion?

Activity: Leaf rubbing and drawing.

Concept: Pattern/shape/texture.

Aim: To make children aware of the outside shapes of leaves and the pattern and texture of the veins.

Resources needed: Any thin, tough white paper, e.g. duplicating or typing paper; scissors; dark wax crayons; pencils; fibre or felt-tip pens.

Preparation: The day before the Session, collect at least two different types of leaf per child. Flatten the leaves by placing them between newspaper and under some heavy books. Choose leaves that have distinct veins and that you know will flatten easily.

Introduction: Give each child a leaf to hold and look at while you talk. Ask what they notice about the leaf. Discuss its outside shape: is it palmate, ovate, lobed, etc? Has it a serrated edge? How would you describe the veins? Do they make a pattern? At what angle do the veins meet the midrib? The emphasis throughout is on *looking* not on how to draw a leaf.

Development: Children may then continue the exploration of the leaf by drawing or making rubbings. Place a leaf on the desk with the veins uppermost and cover it with a piece of paper. Hold the leaf and paper steady with one hand while rubbing firmly with long strokes parallel to the stem. The rubbings may then be cut out ready for mounting.

Evaluation: Did the rubbings clearly describe the pattern and texture made by the veins? Did the drawings indicate that the children have closely observed the shape of the leaf and the texture and pattern of the veins?

Activity: Negative printing.

Concept: Shape.

Aim: To make children aware of the outside shapes of leaves.
To teach the technique of negative printing.

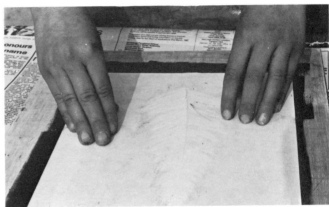

Resources needed: Each group of four or five children will need: printing ink (see page 159); two rollers; a Formica sheet approximately 20 × 30 cm; any fairly absorbent paper; newspaper.

Preparation: The day before the Session, collect at least two different types of leaf or fern per child. Flatten the leaves by placing them between newspaper and under some heavy books. Choose leaves that you know will flatten easily.
Decide where to put prints flat to dry for approximately three hours or string up a washing line and hang prints with paper clips. Do not overlap wet prints.

Introduction: Demonstrate negative printing. Cover tables with newspaper, squeeze about 3 cm of printing ink on to a Formica slab and roll to a perfectly even consistency. The ink must not be sticky or lumpy in places. It should resemble damp velvet. Place the leaf, vein side down, on to the inky surface and cover it with a sheet of white paper. Holding the paper over the leaf with one hand, rub it firmly all over with the other hand. Use only the tips of the fingers and try not to move the paper or leaf. Carefully remove the paper, which should now have a negative or white shape of the leaf in the middle.

Development: If large leaves have been used, the white centre of the negative prints could be used for writing.
When dry, the prints could be the first stage of a pen or pencil drawing. In which case the introduction to Session 71 would be appropriate.

Evaluation: Did the prints clearly show the silhouettes of the leaves?
Was there a fine, even layer of ink on the paper, or was it sticky in places?

Activity: Transfer printing and monoprinting.

Concept: Pattern/shape/texture.

Aim: To consolidate previous work with leaves.
To teach the techniques of transfer and monoprinting.

Resources needed: Each group of four or five children will need: newspaper; printing ink; see page 159; two rollers; a Formica sheet approximately 20 × 30 cm; any fairly absorbent paper, approximately 15 × 20 cm; dustbin.

Preparation: The day before the Session, collect at least two different types of leaf or fern per child. Flatten the leaves by placing them between newspaper and under some heavy books. Choose leaves that you know will flatten easily. Decide where to put prints flat to dry for approximately three hours, or string up a washing line and hang prints with paper clips. Do not overlap wet prints. Cut several sheets of newspaper to approximately 20 × 30 cm.

Introduction: Demonstrate the two processes.
Transfer printing. Cover tables with newspaper. Squeeze about 3 cm of printing ink on to a Formica slab and roll to a perfectly even consistency. The ink must not be sticky or lumpy in places. It should resemble damp velvet. Place the leaf, vein side down, on to the inky surface and cover with a small sheet of newspaper. Holding the stem of the leaf and paper with one hand, rub the paper with the tips of the fingers of the other hand. Rub firmly and carefully where the leaf is but avoid rubbing the background, so as not to remove too much of the ink there. Remove the newspaper and immediately throw it into a dustbin. Holding the stem, carefully remove the leaf from the slab and put it in the centre of the white paper, inky side down. Cover it with another piece of newspaper. Holding the leaf and paper steady with one hand, rub firmly with the other, particularly along the stem and round the edges of the leaf. Remove the newspaper and throw it away. Carefully remove the leaf. There should be a perfect impression of it on the white paper. Put the leaf on to another piece of newspaper, ready to repeat the process. Lie the print flat or hang it up to dry.
Monoprinting. On the Formica slab you should see a faint impression of the leaf. Cover this with a sheet of white paper and rub it all over as hard as possible. Peel off the print and let it dry.

Development: Prints could be cut out and made into a decorative frieze, or used to decorate folder covers, greetings cards, etc.

Evaluation: Did the prints clearly show the shape of the leaves and the pattern and texture of the veins?
Was there a fine, even layer of ink on the paper or was it sticky in places?
Were the children better organised and less messy than in the previous Session?

Activity:	Leaf collage with paper and fabric.
Concept:	Shape.
Aim:	To make children aware of the shapes that occur within the shape of a leaf.

Resources needed: Black paper approximately 20 × 30 cm; paper offcuts or magazines; dark, unpatterned materials approximately 20 × 30 cm; offcuts of materials in light colours; scissors; PVA adhesive and spatulas; chalk; newspaper.

Preparation: Cut paper and/or materials to size.
Cover desks with newspaper and give out the other materials.
Display work produced during Sessions 71, 72, 73.

Introduction: Refer to the work produced during Sessions 71, 72, 73. Children may work from a real leaf or one of their previous drawings or prints. Ask the children to study the shapes outlined by the veins and main stem. Tell them to imagine that the shapes are like pieces of a jigsaw that all fit together.
The first stage is to lightly draw the outline of their leaf with chalk on to black paper or dark materials. This shape should fill the paper. The leaf shape is cut out and the position of the main stem indicated with chalk or pencil. This should be done lightly with a view to rubbing it out later.

Development: Children choose contrasting colours of paper or materials from which they will eventually cut their shapes. Tell them to look carefully at the largest shape outlined by the veins and stem and either to draw and cut it out, or to cut it out without previous drawing. This is placed on to the leaf shape and all the other shapes are similarly cut out and assembled, rather like making a jigsaw, but with small gaps of the background showing to indicate the position of veins and stem. When all the shapes are in position they should be stuck down. Finally, any chalk marks visible should be removed.

Evaluation: Were the children able to draw and cut the shapes?
Were they able to assemble them in the correct positions?

Activity: Tree collage.

Concept: Shape/colour/pattern.

Aim: To consolidate the experience of the previous four Sessions. To learn different drawing techniques.

Resources needed: Some bark; different types of leaves – about two for each child; wax crayons; chalks; green, yellow and orange dye or watery paint; colour magazines; any large backing sheet; cartridge paper; sugar paper; newspaper; brushes; glue; scissors.

Preparation: Cover the tables with newspaper. Cut the sugar and cartridge paper into pieces approximately 15 × 20 cm.
Set up groups as follows:
Group 1. Sugar paper, chalk, leaves.
Group 2. Cartridge paper, wax crayons, leaves.
Group 3. Cartridge paper, wax crayons, dye or runny paint, leaves, brushes.
Group 4. Sugar paper, colour magazines, scissors, glue, leaves.
Group 5. Bark, any large sheets of backing paper; glue.

Introduction: Explain that the object of the session is to produce a group collage of a tree, with the leaves made in different ways. Demonstrate the techniques to be used by each group for making leaves.
Group 1. Chalk drawing. Show how colours may be merged with the fingers.
Group 2. Crayong etching. Leaf colours are applied *heavily* with crayon, leaving no paper showing. A layer of black wax crayon covers up the leaf colours. The black crayon is scraped away to reveal the colours underneath, leaving just black stem and veins.
Group 3. Wax resist. Only the veins and stem are drawn with wax crayons. The leaf is then washed over with dye or runny paint.
Group 4. Paper collage. The shapes of the areas within the veins and stem are cut from magazine pictures and stuck down so that the backing paper shows through for the stem and veins (see Session 74).
Group 5. Any of the above methods to make pieces of bark.

Development: The children carefully draw a leaf shape and then use one of the techniques to make a leaf which is then cut out. Children may make several leaves using the same method or move round the groups. Group 5 is responsible for preparing the backing sheet with a simple outline of branches, and bark stuck on the trunk. This could be pinned up and leaves stuck into position as they are made.

Evaluation: Did the children employ the techniques properly?
Was it apparent that they had studied the shape and colours of the leaves and bark?
Was the collage assembled satisfactorily?

Activity:	Still life design using cut paper.
Concept:	Shape.
Aim:	To make children more aware of the shape of objects and the shapes created by the background.

Resources needed:	Paper, black and three other colours; scissors, adhesive; many different objects with simple silhouette shapes; bottles, keys, etc.; sheet of tracing paper.
Preparation:	Cut black paper to approximately 40 × 30 cm. Hand round scissors. Distribute objects – four objects to a group of about six children.
Introduction:	One by one hold some of the objects against the window with a sheet of tracing paper in front of them. Explain how we recognise some things by their silhouette. Ask children to look carefully at one of their objects, then take it in turns to describe the silhouette while the rest of the class have their eyes shut.
Development:	Ask the children to cut out of coloured paper the silhouette of three objects, and to place the silhouettes on the black background. Cutting should be done directly without preliminary drawing. Explain to the children that they are drawing with scissors. These three shapes should almost fill the paper, but further shapes may be added if necessary until the area of black showing is roughly equivalent to the area of all the coloured shapes. Shapes may overlap if you wish. Arrange the coloured paper until the shapes made by the black background is pleasing or interesting, then fix in position with a little glue.
Evaluation:	Could children describe their shapes verbally? Were the cut shapes easily recognisable? Did pleasing designs result, with interesting background shapes?

Activity: Playground games – frieze.

Concept: Shape.

Aim: To consolidate previous work on silhouettes.

Resources needed:
1. Large sheet of white paper for a background; black paper; scissors; glue.
2. Pictures of figures in silhouette – preferably in action.

Preparation: Cut the black paper to approximately 20 × 10 cm. Hang up the background sheet. Give out glue and scissors. Display results of Session 76.

Introduction: Refer to work done in Session 76. Ask children to recall all the playground games that they can think of and write a list on the board. Ask which ones could be illustrated using only silhouette shapes and tick these. Refer to any pictures of shadow puppets or illustrations where silhouettes have been used, and ask the children what makes for a good silhouette of a figure. Talk about typical postures.

Let the children decide who is going to be responsible for depicting the different playground games, perhaps working in small groups. Explain that in order to arrive at a suitable scale they are cutting their figure from the same sized paper, and that each figure should be that size if they are standing up.

Development: Children may prefer to lightly draw their figures before cutting them out of black paper. As figures are completed they should be pinned on to the prepared background sheet. When all the silhouettes are positioned, a short discussion might ensue to allow suggestions for extra items, improvement of positioning, etc. Finally, the silhouettes should be stuck down.

Evaluation: Did the children produce recognisable figures?
Were there any unexpected results?

Activity: Bonfire night – relief rubbing.

Concept: Shape.

Aim: To encourage expression of an experience through a new medium.
To consolidate work done in the previous Session.

Resources needed:
1. Any cheap paper as a base for sticking shapes; thin white duplicating paper; thin cardboard – e.g. cereal packets; scissors; PVA adhesive.
2. Poems or stories about bonfire night.

Preparation: Display the results of the previous Session.

Introduction: Refer to the work of the previous Session. Read the poems or stories and ask some of the children to describe their own experience of bonfire night. Demonstrate how to make a relief rubbing. Stick a few small cardboard shapes on to a sheet of paper. Place a thin sheet of paper on top and paper-clip the two sheets together. Take a dark wax crayon about 4 cm long and strip off any paper from it. Using the *side* of the crayon, rub firmly over the card shapes.

Development: Invite the children to make a picture of bonfire night by cutting shapes from cardboard, sticking them to a sheet of paper and making a relief rubbing, as demonstrated. After completing the first rubbing, children may wish to add more shapes to the design to make it more interesting. If black wax is used, a wash of yellows and oranges could be applied to the background, finally, to achieve a more dramatic effect.

Evaluation: Did the results convey the excitement of bonfire night.
Did this medium hinder or help expression?
Were some designs more suited to the medium than others, and why?

Activity: Christmas mobiles.

Concept: Pattern/colour/balance.

Aim: To make the children aware of the patterns that exist within a snowflake.
To express snowflake patterns, and use the results as decoration.

Resources needed:
1. Sugar and cartridge paper; scissors; dressmaker's pins; polystyrene tiles; spray diffuser and inks or gold and silver spray aerosols; fixative; PVA adhesive and spatulas; paper doylies; sharp knife.
2. Photographs of snowflakes.

Preparation: Cut the paper to approximately 30 × 30 cm.
Display the photographs of snowflakes.

Introduction: Discuss the snowflakes, pointing out that no two are alike, yet there are definite similarities – they each radiate from a central point and have shapes that repeat.
Suggest to the children that snowflakes might be the theme for the Christmas decorations, and that they should explore a variety of patterns and methods of making them.
Demonstrate a few ways of making snowflake patterns, but encourage the children to develop their own ideas as well.

Development: *Method 1.* Cut the cartridge paper into a circle, approximately 30 cm diameter. Fold in half twice then cut several small shapes from each of the three sides. Fold in half again and cut more shapes. Open out the circle. If necessary, refold and cut more shapes.
Method 2. Cut a design using Method 1 from sugar paper. Pin the design on to a polystyrene tile. Spray with coloured inks, aerosol paint or clear fixative. Remove the sugar paper then repeat the procedure on the reverse side of the tile. Anything with a spirit base will burn into polystyrene leaving a raised surface. The fixative will burn the tile *without* colouring it. If the outside of the tiles are trimmed with a sharp knife, they could be suspended from cotton to form mobiles. Other additions might include the cut paper snowflake stuck on to card of a contrasting colour, or even catering doylies with extra cuts.

Evaluation: Did the results indicate that the children were aware of the patterns within snowflakes?
Were methods employed other than those demonstrated?

Activity: Christmas frieze.

Concept: Line/pattern.

Aim: To encourage the inventive use of line and pattern.

                      See Colour Plate M

Resources needed:
1. Any white paper; felt or fibre-tip pens; crayons; scissors.
2. Poems or stories about the angels visiting the shepherds, e.g. The Nativity in the New Testament, 'Shepherd's Tale' by Steven Ponchon.
3. Pictures of sheep.

Preparation: Cut paper to approximately 20 × 30 cm and 20 × 15 cm.
Put up a large sheet of paper as a background and attach cut paper shapes to suggest hills.

Introduction: Read the poems and stories, and suggest to the children that they might like to make a group picture of the scenes. Divide the class into three groups. Group A will be responsible for the angels, Group B the shepherds and Group C the sheep. When the children have chosen their groups explain that they will be drawing their subject, then cutting it out and pinning it to a large sheet to make a group picture. Shepherds and angels should fill most of the larger sheet and the sheep should fill most of the smaller.

Development: Remind the children of some of their previous work on lines and pattern. Ask the children to decorate the angels' and shepherds' gowns with beautiful patterns consisting of a variety of lines. Some of the patterns could be coloured afterwards if they wish. The sheep should be carefully drawn in black felt-tip and the children should try to convey the texture of the fleece with lines.
As the drawings are completed, children should cut them out and pin them to the backing sheet. When most of the work is up, there should be a brief discussion about the position of the drawings and, if necessary, the drawings should be re-grouped to provide a more pleasing composition.

Evaluation: Did the children pattern their drawings effectively and use line inventively?
Were they ready to suggest improvements to the original positions of the drawings?
Did the children seem to be pleased with the finished results?

Activity: Counter-change patterns.

Concept: Pattern.

Aim: To introduce repeat patterns.

Resources needed:
1. Pencils; black felt-tip pens; rulers; graph paper.
2. Examples of counter-change patterns.

Preparation: Cut up graph paper to approximately 20 × 30 cm. Give out materials.

Introduction: Show the examples of counter-change patterns.
Explain the principle behind repeat printing and how counter-change patterns can be developed. Demonstrate this with a grid drawn on the board. First make a chequered pattern by shading alternate squares. Next divide the squares in half vertically and shade alternate rectangles to produce an elongated chequered pattern. Ask the children to suggest other ways of dividing the squares.

Development: Ask the children to invent their own counter-change patterns. Each pattern should be 7 squares × 7 squares. To start with, suggest that the squares on the graph paper might be divided up with a pencil and ruler to make rectangles, triangles, etc., which are easy to fill in with felt tips and to repeat. When at least two patterns have been completed in this way, the children could then go on to devise patterns by breaking the graph down with curved lines drawn freehand, and filling in these shapes.

Evaluation: Did the children produce counter-change patterns?
Did the children invent their own patterns?
Were there any quite original designs?

Activity: Inventive symmetry.

Concept: Pattern.

Aim: To make the children aware of symmetry in nature.
To allow practice at inventing symmetrical designs.

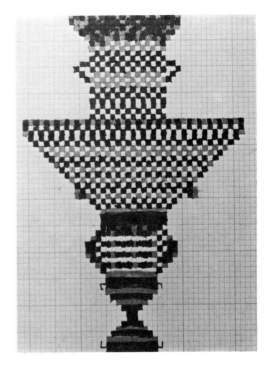

Resources needed:
1. Fine graph paper; felt or fibre-tip pens; coloured pencils.
2. Any pictures that illustrate symmetry in nature.

Preparation: Display the results of the previous Session.
Cut graph paper to approximately 10 × 15 cm.
Give out pens or coloured pencils.

Introduction: Refer to the work displayed from the previous Session, and praise any unusual or imaginative patterns. Ask if anyone knows what a symmetrical pattern or design is. Can anyone give examples from nature? Show pictures illustrating symmetry and explain the principle involved – a butterfly is a good example. Ask the children if they notice anything about the markings on the wings. Point out that the colours, shapes, patterns, etc., on one wing correspond exactly to those on the opposite wing. That is what symmetry implies. Demonstrate how to invent your own symmetrical designs on graph paper folded down the centre. Whichever squares are filled in on one side of the crease must correspondingly be filled in on the other.

Development: Ask the children to practise on a small piece of graph paper using just one colour. Once they understand the basic principle, suggest that they might like to invent a symmetrical creature, robot, rocket ship or abstract design, using several colours.

Evaluation: Did the results suggest that the children understood the principle of symmetry?
Were there any original or inventive designs?

Activity:	Studying radial designs.
Concept:	Pattern/line.
Aim:	To make children aware of radial designs in nature. To increase children's powers of concentration and observation.

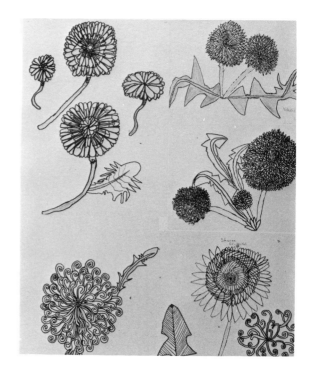

Resources needed:	1. Any cheap drawing paper; felt or fibre-tip pens; pencils. 2. As many examples as possible of plants with radial designs such as the common daisy or dandelion.
Preparation:	Cut paper to approximately 20 × 30 cm. Give out plants, pens and pencils.
Introduction:	Ask the children what the plants have in common. Explain that, with any radiating design, the shapes of individual elements like petals all seem to be moving outwards from the same central point. Ask some of the children to point out any unusual or interesting features about their plant, and the rest of the class should check their own plant for similarities. After this preliminary discussion, children should be encouraged to make analytical drawings that describe the structure of the plant, with particular attention paid to the way in which parts radiate from a central point.
Development:	Ask the children to draw larger than life size. After very lightly sketching in the general shape of the plant with a pencil, ask them to work in felt or fibre-tip pen. They may draw just part of the plant or the whole plant, but the object is to show how one part joins on to another, slowly building up a radial pattern.
Evaluation:	Did the results indicate that the children had closely studied the plants?

Activity:	Radial mosaics
Concept:	Pattern/texture.
Aim:	To consolidate previous work on radial designs. To encourage the imaginative use of everyday materials.

Resources needed:
1. Stiff paper or thin card, preferably dark; PVA adhesive and spatulas; variety of materials suitable for textured, edible collage, e.g. lentils, pasta, breakfast cereals; circular objects for drawing around, diameter approximately 10 cm.
2. Photographs of snakes.

Preparation: Ask children to bring in some edible collage materials.
Cut paper into squares approximately 15 × 15 cm and distribute materials.

Introduction: Show photographs and discuss the patterns normally found on snakes. What do the children know about snakes? Remind them of snakes that eat animals whole. Ask them if snakes are edible and invite them to make an imaginary edible snake, working as a group.
Remind the class about the previous session on radials, and explain that the markings of this snake are based on radial patterns, but all different.

Development: Take a paper square and draw a circle lightly in pencil. Put a dot in the centre. Make radial patterns by sticking the lentils, etc. to the paper. To display the finished circles, they could be cut out and stuck on to a previously prepared snake shape.

Evaluation: Did the children remember much about the radial patterns from Session 83?
Were the radial patterns produced, imaginative?

Activity: Tie and dye.

Concept: Pattern/colour.

Aim: To consolidate the concept of radial designs.
To introduce a new medium.

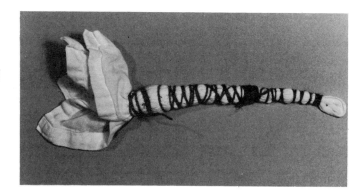

Resources needed: Offcuts of white or light-coloured cotton materials; any dark Dylon cold water dye; rubber gloves; salt; soda; two buckets or large bowls; mixing spoons; newspapers.

Preparation: Display the results of the previous two Sessions.
Dye Bucket: dissolve two level teaspoonsful of dye in half a litre of warm water.
Fixative Bucket: dissolve four tablespoons of common salt and one tablespoon of household soda in half a litre of hot water.
Allow solution in both buckets to cool, then mix both solutions together. Once mixed, this dyebath is effective for a maximum of three hours.
Each child will need at least one piece of material approximately 15 × 15 cm, several pieces of string approximately 20 cm long and a sheet of newspaper. Tell the children to put their initials in biro in one corner of the material.

Introduction: Refer to the radial designs of the previous Sessions, and tell the children that they will be making similar designs by the tie and dye method. Explain and demonstrate the technique. Take a square of material about 15 × 15 cm. Hold the centre with thumb and finger of one hand and allow the rest of the material to fall in fairly even folds. Wrap the 20 cm of string tightly round the material and tie a double knot. Wet the material thoroughly and squeeze out excess water. Immerse the wet material in the dye bath for about 30 minutes, stirring occasionally. Lift it up with a stick and squeeze out surplus dye using rubber gloves. Put the dyed material on to a sheet of newspaper and carry it to the sink or bucket of water. Rinse the material thoroughly, then squeeze out surplus water. Undo the string and show the pattern.

Development: Children may prefer to work in pairs, one holding the folds of material even while the partner ties the first knot. There are no set rules about tying. The string could cover the material in a criss-cross fashion in one piece or be cut up and used to bind the material in separate bands. The essential requirement, however, is that the binding should be *tight* otherwise the dye will creep under the string and there will be little or no pattern.
Finished designs could have the edges stitched and be used as a decorative mat for vases.

Evaluation: Did the children enjoy this activity?
Did they produce radial designs?

Activity:	Drawing hands and finger prints.
Concept:	Line.
Aim:	To increase powers of observation.

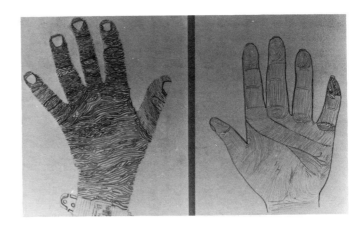

Resources needed:	Pencils; ball-point pens; fibre and felt-tip pens; any white paper.
Preparation:	Cut paper to approximately 20×30 cm.
Introduction:	Ask children to study the palm of the hand that they do not normally write with. Ask which are the main lines and the directions they take. Invite discussion and encourage appropriate adjectives and metaphors to describe the lines: e.g. jagged furrows that plough through the skin like a river through a valley.
Development:	Children should place their hand, palm facing up, on to their paper and lightly draw the outline with a pencil. They should then choose one of the pens to draw all the lines on their hands, starting with the deep ones and gradually working down to the fine ones.
Evaluation:	Were they able to use appropriate adjectives to describe the lines? For how long did they concentrate on their drawings? Did the results indicate careful observation?

Activity:	Silhouette profiles.
Concept:	Shape.
Aim:	To make the children aware of the shape and proportions of a human head.

Resources needed: Black paper; scrap white paper; pencils; scissors; paste; brushes; white backing paper. Old picture frame covered with tracing paper approximately 40 × 30 cm.

Preparation: Cut all the paper to approximately 20 × 30 cm. Give each child a sheet of white scrap paper and a sheet of black, chalk and scissors.

Introduction: Ask a child to stand sideways close to a window, so that the rest of the class is seeing him or her in profile. Put the tracing paper frame in front of the child so that he/she now appears in silhouette. Ask the class questions designed to make them aware of the proportions of the head and characteristic features. Can we still recognise the person? Which features do we instantly recognise? Could you describe the general shape of the head? Where do the eyes, nose and mouth come in relation to the chin and the top of the head? What shape is the nose, etc.?

Development: Ask the children to work in pairs. One sits sideways to his partner, preferably against the background of a window or white wall, while the other attempts to draw a profile outline of the head. Tell the children to ignore the inside features, like eyes and ears, but to concentrate on proportions and general shape. Start by lightly drawing the general shape, which should fill the paper.
After a trial run on white paper, go on to the black paper using chalk. When both partners have a chalk drawing on black paper, ask them to cut away the background and mount the silhouette on to a white background.

Evaluation: Did the children manage to get the general shape and proportions of the head? Was it possible to recognise the sitter in some cases?

Activity:	Portraits.
Concept:	Shape/proportion.
Aim:	To consolidate the work of the previous Session. To make the children more aware of the shape and proportions of a human head.

Resources needed: Any sort of paper; pencils; chalk; crayons; rulers.

Preparation: Display the work of the previous Session. Cut paper to approximately 26 × 30 cm. Put out a range of drawing materials.

Introduction: Refer to the work of the previous Session and praise the efforts of those who had managed to get the proportions about right, even though the sitter is unrecognisable. Ask a child to stand next to the blackboard, facing the class. Recap on proportions and demonstrate on the blackboard. Measure the child's head from the top to the chin. Announce the measurement and draw an oval about this size on the board. Ask the class how many centimetres do they think it is from the top of the head to the eyes, tip of the nose and mouth. Take these measurements and lightly mark the oval on the board to indicate the positions.

Development: Ask the children to take the same approach to draw a life-size portrait of their friend. After they have lightly drawn the shape of the head and marked the position of the three main features, tell them to closely observe details and to record them carefully.

Evaluation: Did the children improve on the previous session on the general shape and proportion of the head? Was it possible to recognise the sitter in some cases?

Activity: Hair.

Concept: Line.

Aim: To increase the children's powers of observation and concentration.

Resources needed: Any white paper; pencils, fibre or felt-tip pens; pen and ink.

Preparation: Display the work of the previous Session. Cut paper to approximately 20 × 30 cm.

Introduction: Refer to the work of the previous Session. Ask if any of the portraits are recognisable. Then ask if they could recognise their best friend if they could only see the back of his/her head. Is everyone different from the back view? What is different about them? Ask the children to study the back of one another's heads and to describe exactly how the hair grows. Using a similar approach to the previous session, ask the children to observe the general shape of the head, viewed from the back, and to draw it lightly in pencil about full size.

Development: Tell the children to attempt to draw every hair on the person's head, making sure that the direction of growth is correct, for that is what will give this portrait its distinctive features. Use a fibre or felt-tip pen, or pen and ink.

Evaluation: Did the results indicate that the children had closely observed their subject?

Activity: Class portrait.

Concept: Colour/shape/proportion.

Aim: To consolidate work of the previous Session.
To allow practice in colour matching and mixing.

Resources needed: Light grey sugar paper; painting materials; pencils or chalk; newspaper.

Preparation: Display work of Session 89. Cut paper to approximately 30 × 40 cm. Cover tables with newspaper and give out painting materials.

Introduction: Refer to the work of Session 89 and discuss the relative success of the children to overcome the problems of proportion.
Explain that you would like the children to do a painted portrait this time, trying to get the colours as close to real life as possible. Demonstrate how to mix unusual or subtle colours, e.g. hair.
1. Ask someone with light brown hair to step forward.
2. Mix black and white together in a palette until you think that the resultant grey is the same tone, in other words as dark as the hair. Test the paint on a scrap of paper and hold it against the hair. Does it need more white or black, or is it the same tone exactly.
3. When you have achieved the correct tone, ask the children which colours might be added to the grey to make it the same as the hair colour.
4. Add small amounts of brown until you have a good match, then adjust the tone by adding white or black.

Development: Ask the children to approach the portrait in the same way as they did their previous portrait, by lightly drawing in the shape of the head and marking in the position of the three main features, nose, eyes and mouth. Tell them not to bother with painting the background as the portraits will be cut out and mounted as a class portrait.

Evaluation: Were proportions better than those of the previous Session and was there more attention to detail?
Did the children match colours satisfactorily?
Were there any good likenesses?

Stages 5 and 6 – upper juniors

Each stage comprises fifteen Sessions, allowing for about five Sessions each term. Each Session aims to either introduce or increase awareness of an artistic concept or concepts, which are stated at the beginning of each Session outline. Hopefully, teachers will augment these Sessions with others that will further increase awareness of these concepts, and also allow children time to develop newly-acquired skills.

Much of the work of these stages will be concerned with developing experiences gained at previous stages. It is essential, therefore, that teachers should know what experiences the children have already had.

In the final stage children are beginning to 'see' the world as an adult does, and tend to become discouraged because their work does not 'look right'. Children's work should not be judged in adult terms, but praised as being valid for that particular child. Crafts may be developed from different levels, and it might be pointed out that their rather simplistic way of creating has parallels in the adult world, and that this work is greatly admired in its own right – masks, totem poles, African carving, barge painting and work by modern primitive or naive painters.

Stage 5

Stage 6

Activity: Studying natural form.

Concept: Texture.

Aim: To consolidate previous work in texture.
To increase children's awareness of texture in natural form.

Resources needed:

1. Any light coloured paper approximately 20×30 cm; pieces of bark; any paper approximately 10×10 cm for viewfinders; pins or Blutack; scissors; charcoal, crayons, pens, fibre or felt-tip pens; ink; twigs, etc.
2. Pictures of different types of textured surfaces found in nature.

Preparation: Previous to this Session, ask children to collect pieces of bark. Cut paper to size. Practise making marks with a twig dipped into ink.

Introduction: Discuss the meaning of texture and how it differs from pattern. Refer to examples in nature and show pictures that invite a variety of words to describe the texture; silky, coarse, rough, jagged, hairy, etc. Hand round pieces of bark and discuss them with reference to surface quality. How could we express some of these qualities without words? Demonstrate the use of sharpened twigs dipped into ink, charcoal, etc. Demonstrate how to make a viewfinder by folding the smaller paper in half and cutting out a rectangle approximately 3×4 cm. Alternatively, the frames of unwanted 35 mm slides could be used.

Development: The children make a viewfinder. This is moved across their piece of bark until an interesting arrangement of shapes and textures is framed. The viewfinder is fixed in that position with pins or Blutack and the children draw what they see within the frame. The drawing, which should completely fill the paper, should correspond with whatever can be seen in the viewfinder. Any drawing medium is permitted which adequately describes the texture of the bark, but for this session pencils should be discouraged.

Evaluation: Could the children verbally differentiate between pattern and texture?
Did their drawings adequately express textural quality?

Activity: Interpreting bark – collage.

Concept: Texture/shape/colour.

Aim: To increase children's powers of observation.
To consolidate work of the previous Session.
To allow experimentation with collage materials.

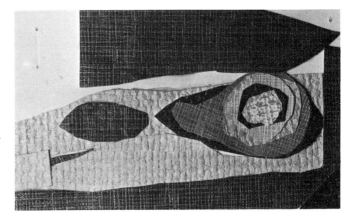

Resources needed: Pieces of bark; viewfinders made for the previous Session; pins or Blutack; scissors; PVA adhesive; any backing paper for collage.
Collage materials that could be used to express the colours and texture of bark: paper offcuts, fabric, wallpaper, sawdust, soil, etc. These materials should preferably be sorted according to colour and put into separate boxes.

Preparation: Display drawings done during the previous Session.
Ask the children to bring in some of the collage materials needed.

Introduction: Hand out pieces of bark.
Refer to the drawings on display and particularly to those that expressed well the *textural* quality of the bark.
Explain that this Session will be concerned with expressing the bark's other chief characteristics – colour and shape.
Ask the children to study their piece of bark and to notice the way in which it is broken up into lots of shapes, just like a jigsaw puzzle, except that sometimes the shapes overlap one another. Discuss the colours and ask the children to count the different colours they can see, and then how many shades of one colour they can see.

Development: Ask the children to use their viewfinder to isolate one small part of the bark. The viewfinder is then fixed in that position with pins or Blutack.
Ask the children to choose from the materials available, those that best match in colour and texture the main shapes that appear within the viewfinder; then to cut them out carefully and place them on the backing sheet. They may greatly enlarge the shapes or work life-size. When most of the shapes have been placed in position they should be stuck down.

Evaluation: Did the results indicate that the children had taken care to choose appropriate colours and textures?
Were there any other interesting observations?

Activity:	Studying texture: plaster casts.
Concept:	Texture.
Aim:	To consolidate previous work on texture. To increase the children's awareness of texture in nature. To introduce children to casting.

Resources needed: Plasticine, about 225 gm each; piece of bark each; card strip approximately 35 × 4 cm; boot polish; plaster of Paris, about 110 gm for each cast; plastic mixing bowl; rolling pins or pieces of broom handle; sticky tape.

Preparation: Make your own plaster cast in order to iron out any little snags.

Introduction: Remind children of the discussion that introduced Session 91 and refer to some of the results of that Session. Demonstrate how to make a plaster cast from a piece of bark.

Development: On a smooth surface roll out Plasticine until it is roughly 8 × 12 cm and at least 1 cm thick throughout. Turn it over so that the smooth side is uppermost. Gently but firmly press the bark into the Plasticine, then carefully peel the Plasticine off and place it flat on the desk with the impression of the bark facing up. Bend the cardboard strip into the required shape (rectangle, circle, oval) and stick the ends with tape. Press the card into the Plasticine so that it makes a wall about 3 cm high around the most interesting part of the impression. You are now ready for the plaster. Follow the directions on page 159 then pour the plaster into the mould to a depth of about 1 cm. Thump the desk top with the fist to eliminate air bubbles. While waiting for the plaster to set, children could be preparing another mould, perhaps using a leaf instead of bark. After about thirty minutes it should be safe to gently peel off the Plasticine and card and to trim any untidy edges with a blunt knife. The plaster cast is then ready for a light wash of water-colour or a wipe over with boot polish to enhance the texture.

Evaluation: Did the children produce casts that clearly showed the texture of the bark? Did they handle the materials properly?

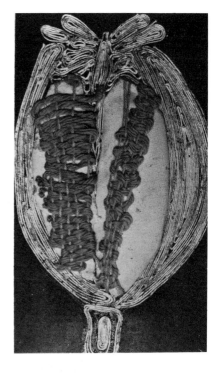

Activity: Studying pods.

Concept: Texture/shape.

Aim: To consolidate previous work on texture and shape. To encourage the inventive use of materials. To increase children's awareness of texture and shape in natural form.

Resources needed:
1. Strong backing paper or card approximately 25 × 15 cm; offcuts of string, wool, raffia, material, etc. but only in similar or natural colours; PVA adhesive and spatulas.
2. Pictures of plants that have pods. Real examples of plants with pods, e.g. poppies.

Preparation: Previous to this Session ask the children to collect any plants that have pods, and also offcuts of string, etc. Cut paper to size. Display results of Session 92 and also pictures of plants with pods.

Introduction: Refer to work of Session 93, where just one small part of the bark was focused upon. This time we shall look at the shapes and textures that make up a complete plant. Discuss the pictures on display and also the pods brought in by the children. Ask them to describe the total shape of the pod and then any shapes found within that shape. Then describe the different surface textures and discuss how these might be expressed with the available materials.

Development: Children should cut out of material the main shapes seen on the pod and stick these to the backing paper or card. Cutting should be direct with little or no preliminary drawing. Surface texture may then be expressed by choosing appropriate materials and sticking these to the main shapes. As an alternative, if the backing were hessian or another plain weave, shapes could be stitched to it and surface textures could be expressed with wool or cotton stitches. As well as using traditional tacking, running or chain stitches, children might also be encouraged to invent their own forms of sewing which are appropriate to describing different textures.

Evaluation: Did the finished collages have something of the plant's character? Was textural quality expressed imaginatively?

Activity:	Calendars.
Concept:	Design/composition.
Aim:	To arrive at a satisfactory arrangement of leaves that fits the shape of the calendar.

Resources needed:

1. Well before this Session it is necessary to collect about six different types of leaf for each child. The leaves should be placed carefully between newspaper so as not to overlap, then stored under some heavy books.
2. Thin white card, approximately 20 × 20 cm; PVA adhesive and spatulas; small calendars and tape for attaching them; card or wool for hanging; transparent self-adhesive sheeting; compasses; pencils; scissors.
3. Examples of designs within a circle or oval, e.g. Victorian Christmas cards and flower paintings.

Preparation: Sort out the leaves into families. Give out four different leaves to each child. Give out the card, compasses, pencils and scissors.

Introduction: Show the children examples of designs within a circle or oval and ask which ones seem to fit the shape well. What things do they like or dislike about the designs? Ask the children to draw a circle that fills the white card and then to cut it out. Tell them to place their four leaves within the circle to make a pleasing design that seems to be suitable for the shape. After initial trials, children may decide to add or take away leaves from their designs.

Development: When children have found a pleasing arrangement, tell them to stick down their leaves with PVA.
Designs may be made more permanent by covering with transparent, self-adhesive sheeting. Finally attach the small calendar to the bottom of the design with sticky tape and the cord at the top for hanging.

Evaluation: Did the arrangements seem to fit comfortably within the circles?
Did the designs have a feeling of composition, with the shapes that were big, balanced by several small shapes?

Activity: Red Indian masks.

Concept: Pattern/colour.

Aim: To produce symmetrical
                 designs for masks, similar in
                 style to those made by Red
                 Indians.

Resources   1. Sugar paper approximately 20 × 30 cm; painting materials; offcuts of fabric and paper;
needed: PVA adhesive and spatulas; newspaper; scissors.
                 2. Pictures and slides of Red Indians and a projector.

Preparation: Cover tables with newspaper.
                 Set up projector.

Introduction: Show slides and pictures. Discuss the culture of the Indians, their way of life before the white
                 settlers arrived. Pay particular attention to the clothes worn, decoration and colours used.
                 Refer to any pictures of masks and discuss how and why they were used.
                 Ask the children to design and make their own mask that might be used at a war dance. They
                 should think carefully about the colours that they will choose in order to give the most
                 startling or frightening effects. The children may use as much decoration as they like, but the
                 designs should be symmetrical, and not copied from the pictures shown.

Development: Tell the children to cut out an oval or rectangular shape from their paper. They may then add
                 decoration in any way – by painting or collage, or a combination of both perhaps.

Evaluation: Were the designs frightening and warlike?
                 Did the children remember to make symmetrical designs?
                 Did the children simply copy the pictures or were there any original designs?

Activity: Red Indian woven designs.

Concept: Pattern/colour.

Aim: To design symmetrical patterns based on the square or diamond.

Resources needed:
1. Graph paper with very small squares; felt-tip pens.
2. Pictures and slides of Red Indians.
3. A projector.

Preparation: Set up projector.
Display results of the previous Session.

Introduction: Show slides and pictures. Discuss the decoration used for clothing and explain that this would have been made by simple weaving methods. Point out that most of the designs are symmetrical and based on square or diamond shapes.

Development: Ask the children to design a length of braid to be worn by an important chief. Designs should be based on a square or diamond, be symmetrical and should repeat at least three times. The final pattern should be rich and colourful.
As the final result would be woven, designs should be worked out in terms of the small graph paper squares. Children may either attempt to copy designs seen in the pictures or they can invent their own designs.

Evaluation: Were the designs symmetrical?
Did the children attempt to copy designs seen in the pictures or did they invent their own?
Were there any original or unusual results?

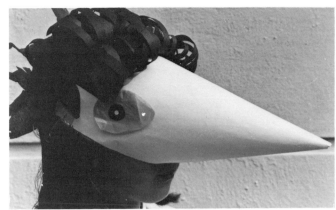

Activity: Masks for drama.

Concept: Colour/pattern.

Aim: To consolidate previous work
                     on designing masks.
                     To practise paper sculpting
                     techniques.

Resources   1. Pictures and slides of masks used for drama, including pictures of tribal masks. If the masks
needed: are to be used for a specific production, provide pictures for inspiration.
                     2. Human masks; thin card; rulers; pencils; PVA adhesive; spatulas; stapler; paper offcuts.
                     3. Bird masks are described in Session 54.

Preparation: Cut the card to approximately 20×30 cm.
                     Display the pictures of masks, plus any other inspirational material.

Introduction: Discuss the purpose of making the mask and point to examples of masks that have been used
                     for similar purposes.
                     Demonstrate how to make the base of the mask in the four stages illustrated in Session 54. If
                     the wearer of the mask needs to speak, it is advisable to cut away the bottom half of the mask.
                     Attach a piece of string to each side of the mask ready for tying round the back of the head.

Development: When adding features to their masks, children should greatly exaggerate the main features so
                     that they can be seen from a distance. Offcuts of coloured paper may be useful for adding
                     eyebrows, mouth and nose (see the method for making the beak – Session 54). Whiskers, hair
                     and eyelashes can be made by cutting thin strips of paper. These can be curled by gently
                     pulling each strip between the thumb and the blade of a pair of scissors.

Evaluation: Were the masks well made?
                     Could the character of the mask be recognised from at least ten metres?
                     Were previous skills consolidated and new ones tried?

Activity: Spontaneous puppetry – glove puppets.

Concept: Form/shape/colour.

Aim: To encourage group co-operation to produce a puppet production.
To encourage an experimental approach to making puppets.

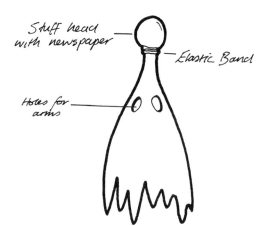

Stuff head with newspaper

Elastic Band

Holes for arms

Resources needed: Circles of plain material or tissue paper approximately 40 cm in diameter; newspaper; elastic bands or string; PVA adhesive; spatulas; fabric and paper offcuts; boxes, yoghurt cartons, etc. suitable for animal heads; old tights; blanket; length of wood approximately 4 cm × 4 cm × 2 m; drawing pins.

Preparation: Make a puppet theatre by tacking a blanket to a length of wood. If this is supported by two cupboards or tables, the puppeteers can crouch behind out of sight.

Introduction: Divide the class into groups of four or five. Ask them to think of a story that they all know that would take about three minutes to tell, perhaps a fairy tale. Ideally, the story should have the same number of characters in it as there are in the group, but this is not vital. Having decided on the story, the children should then decide who is going to be responsible for a particular character(s), which will be depicted by a glove puppet. Tell the children to consider the personality of their character and to exaggerate any peculiarities – a very long hooked nose, pointed chin for a witch, etc. Explain that speed and simplicity are essential and that whereas any of the waste materials supplied may be utilised it is suggested that the method illustrated be used for making human characters. Session 100 describes a method for making animals.

Development: Set a time limit for making the puppets – say 45 minutes. Allow about ten minutes for a practice, then ask each group in turn to put on their puppet production. Explain that each puppet should do its own speaking or growling or grunting and that the story should be clear *without* the use of a narrator. Simple, hand-held props or scenery is permissible but children should generally avoid scenery.

Evaluation: Did everyone seem to enjoy this Session?
Did the children co-operate as a group?
Did they use the materials imaginatively?

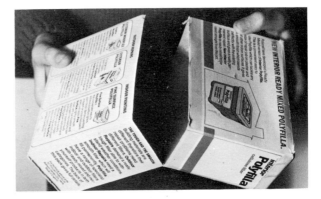

Activity: Box puppetry.

Concept: Form/shape/colour.

Aim: To allow practice in modelling
                   a character.
                   To allow practice in designing
                   and making costumes.

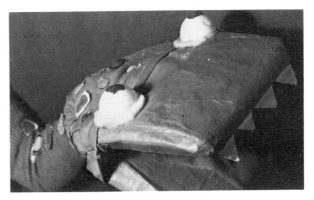

Resources needed: A cardboard box, the dimensions of a small washing powder carton; an old pair of tights or a woollen jumper; table tennis ball; PVA adhesive; stapler; fabric offcuts; newspaper; paste; painting materials.

Preparation: As this explains a particular method of making a puppet, the preparation and introduction of Session 99 would also apply here.

Introduction: This method is particularly useful for any characters requiring large, moveable mouths, e.g. snake, dragon, lion, troll, ogre, giant, etc.

Development: Cut the cardboard box along three sides as shown. Bend the box back and insert the fingers into the top section and the thumb into the bottom.
                    Take a tube of stretchy material cut from the arm of an old jumper or the leg of a pair of tights and stretch one end of the tube around the head of your puppet (i.e. the box, which can now be operated as a mouthpiece). Staple the tube around the back of the head in about four places and use PVA to glue it into position. Add more staples if necessary.
                    For speedy, spontaneous productions as described in Session 99, it is now only necessary to cover the box with paint or pasted paper. Should a more substantial puppet be required, however, and more time is available, this is the next step. Additional features such as eyes made from table tennis balls cut in half, should be stuck on with PVA. With the fabric tube firmly in position, cover all visible cardboard with two layers of pasted paper – one of newspaper and one of kitchen paper. See the notes on page 154.
                    If the puppet is not to be painted, a finishing layer of tissue paper could be pasted down.
                    The body of the puppet – the tube – can now be decorated with fabric offcuts stuck or sewn into position. If necessary, arms could be attached and a length of galvanised wire sewn to each hand will allow the puppet to make gestures.

Activity: Silhouette compositions.

Concept: Shape/colour/composition.

Aim: To consolidate previous work in silhouettes and colour. To compose a picture using existing images.

See Colour Plate E

Resources needed:
1. Sugar paper; black paper; scissors; pencils; painting materials; newspaper.
2. Pictures where silhouette shapes are seen against the setting sun. Plenty of picture books and magazines.

Preparation: Cut paper to approximately 30 × 40 cm. Prepare the room for painting.

Introduction: Show children the pictures of sunsets. Discuss the colours in the sky and how they merge into one another. Discuss the silhouette forms, and how black they appear against the light sky.

Development: Invite the children to make a composition which features silhouette forms against a sunset sky, and suggest the following stages.
1. Mix the appropriate colours and completely cover the paper with a sunset sky, remembering to merge in the colours.
2. Go through the books and magazines and choose an appropriate subject.
3. Using only black paint and starting low down on the paper paint in a skyline in silhouette. This could be imagined or taken from real life or from photographs.
4. Using the magazine pictures as a guide, draw silhouette shapes on to black paper, then cut them out. About three or four shapes will be needed.
5. Position the shapes against the sky to make an interesting arrangement, grouping them so that the background shapes are also pleasing. Aim for some sort of balance between busy areas and blank space. In other words, do not fill every bit of space up by spreading shapes out or having too many.
6. Encourage discussion amongst friends before finally sticking down the shapes.

Evaluation: Were the children able to mix and lay the appropriate colours for the background? Were their silhouette shapes recognisable? Were pictures composed with due regard to shapes left in the background and balance of shapes and space left?

Activity: Complementary colours.

Concept: Colour.

Aim: To make children aware of the disjointed or jarring effect of complementary colours, or too many colours, in a picture.

Resources needed:
1. Any painting paper; newspaper; painting materials; colour circle – this could be taken from the children's folder (Session 51).
2. Reproductions of paintings where the artist has used complementary colours to create a jarring effect, e.g. Matisse, Derain, Picasso, Van Gogh.

Preparation: Cut paper to approximately 30 × 40 cm. Prepare the room for painting. Display the results of the previous Session.

Introduction: Refer to the work on display where the colour has been used to create a harmonious effect. This has been achieved by using only those colours close to one another in the colour circle. Point this out on a colour circle. Explain that the aim of this Session is to create an effect with colour that is the opposite of harmonious – disjointed or jarring. Ask which colours would be appropriate to choose from the colour circle. Those colours directly opposite to one another in the colour circle are best, e.g. blue and orange, red and green, yellow and violet. Discuss the colours in the reproductions.

Development: Tell the children to paint the silhouette of a tree with black. Only the main branches need be painted and these should extend to the edge of the paper. Ask the children to choose two *complementary* colours – opposites in the colour circle. The sky behind the tree should be painted mainly in those two colours, but others could be introduced also. Keep reminding the children what the main aim of the Session is – to create a jarring effect with colour. If time allows, discuss the results.

Evaluation: Did the paintings lack harmony and appear disjointed because of the choice of colours?

Activity:　　　Images to music.

Concept:　　　Colour/shape.

Aim:　　　To allow experimentation with a new medium.
To encourage the children to interpret music visually.

Resources needed:　1. 35 mm slide mounts (obtainable from any photographic dealer); Cellophane paper; coloured inks; scissors; drinking straws; slide projector and screen; record player or tape recorder, and appropriate music, e.g. *Peer Gynt* by Grieg.

Preparation:　　Set up projector and record player or tape recorder. Play music through and note where the changes of mood occur. Time each of these sections. Allowing ten seconds for each slide, work out how many slides may be viewed during each section, e.g. a section lasting thirty seconds will have three slides allocated to it.

Introduction:　　Ask the children to close their eyes while the music is being played and to try to remember certain parts of the music that bring to mind particular colours. After playing the music through, tell the children that the music will be played again, but this time it will be stopped in certain places when the mood of the music changes. When it stops the first time, children should write number 1, then to jot down any colour and shape or movement that came to mind, e.g. blues and greens, spiky and jerky. Tell them to write notes for each part of the music as it stops. When the music finishes, ask the children to choose just one section that they particularly enjoyed. Write the section numbers on the board and alongside the initials of those children who have chosen that section. Try to spread the numbers in each section, ensuring that they correspond with your initial calculations for each section, allowing ten seconds for each slide.

Development:　　Explain that the class will collaborate to make a slide presentation to accompany the music. Each child should start by making a slide to suit his particular section of the music. Two rectangles of clear or coloured Cellophane should be cut to fit neatly into the slide mount. The design is made either by cutting and sticking other pieces of Cellophane and/or dropping blobs of the appropriate coloured inks on to one of the rectangles of Cellophane. All shapes should be kept simple and of an abstract nature and there should be no attempts to illustrate. Children will probably produce several slides, although only one slide mount is needed. After viewing their efforts through a hand viewer or projector set up in a dark corner or under a table, they can modify and discard accordingly before deciding on their final version. As slides are completed they should be put in order according to the section of the music to which they relate. Slides are projected at ten second intervals while the music is playing.

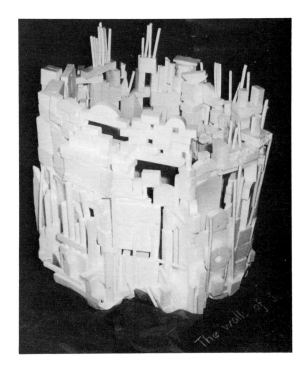

Activity: Inventing with waste.

Concept: Form/texture/shape.

Aim: To encourage children to use waste materials imaginatively.

Resources needed: Waste materials of any kind. It is surprising how much first class model-making material is discarded by shops and factories. The teacher's task is to arrange collection (or delivery) and then categorise and store it in suitable boxes. One system is to have a collection of labelled shoe boxes with different items in each. These could be stacked in an odd store place, and replenished periodically by the children. Schools that make it known to parents that they are grateful to receive factory waste, very quickly find their stock cupboard full of unlikely but useful *free* materials.

Preparation: It is as well to know how to stick together a variety of materials and the notes on page 157 might come in useful. It is always best, whenever possible, to organise materials in such a way that children know exactly what is available. See waste materials on page 160.

Introduction: Two different approaches are suggested:
1. Produce materials that could provide the starting point to several quite different projects, e.g. a box of polystyrene shapes used for packing. The children might simply be asked What could you make with this? The teacher might provide suggestions as a stimulus or give an open-ended design-brief such as make a construction of at least 20 × 20 cm base area and not less than 20 cm high. The children simply use their ingenuity, but are offered assistance with construction.
2. Use the rolled-paper method of constructing a base for making animals (see Session 37). Older children can put a piece of galvanised wire inside each roll, so that limbs will stay in position. Then choose from any materials available to suggest fur, scales, skin, etc. These should be cut up and stuck to the base, to make the animal as realistic as possible. Work from real animals or photographs.

Development: The photograph illustrates one approach. The polystyrene suggested the walls of Jericho, which were built up and stuck together with PVA adhesive.

Activity:	Problem-solving constructions.
Concept:	Linear structure.
Aim:	To present a design problem that has several possible solutions.

Resources needed:
1. Construction straws or drinking straws.
2. Photographs of constructions based upon the triangle, e.g. bridges, Eiffel tower, etc.
3. Impact adhesive, e.g. Evostick.

Introduction:
Show photographs and discuss their construction. Ask the children what they notice about each construction. How do they think the designer first started?
Explain that the class will be divided into groups of three or four and will all work on the same problem: to build a construction at least two metres high, made from only whole straws and adhesive. The winning team will be the one using the least number of straws, the method of joining will be the same for everyone.
Demonstrate this by flattening the ends of two straws and dipping them into the adhesive – only a thin smear is necessary. When the glue is thoroughly dry, bring the two ends together, which will join on impact.

Development:
Tell the children to prepare about twenty straws with adhesive and to lie these side by side on a desk, making sure that the ends do not touch. After about ten minutes they should be ready to use. Allow time for discussion.

Evaluation:
Did every group manage to produce a satisfactory solution?
Were some stronger than others?
Which were more elegant or pleasing to the eye?

Activity:	Studying the environment.
Concept:	Line/pattern/shape.
Aim:	To encourage children to observe closely and to record accurately.

Resources needed: Sketchbooks or clipboard with bulldog clips; paper approximately 20 × 30 cm; felt, ball-point and fibre-tip pens; pencils; viewfinders.

Preparation: Viewfinders could be simply made by removing the film from unwanted 35 mm slides, or cutting a rectangular hole about 3 × 2 cm in a piece of thin card about 6 × 4 cm.

Introduction: Before taking children outside, be specific about the subject being studied and suggest ways in which it might be tackled. If, for example, the school building is to be the subject, take the children round the outside and ask them to make notes of all the examples of pattern to be found – brickwork, slates, railings, etc. Tell the children to make thumbnail sketches of each plus written notes. The object of this exercise is to build up as much information as possible. A time limit of, say, five minutes might be set for each location so that, in half-an-hour, children have to find and make notes on pattern in six different parts of the building.

Development: Next, children might be asked to use their viewfinders, held about 30 cm from their eyes, to isolate one example of pattern on the building. Whatever can be seen through the viewfinder should appear on the paper. Children must be encouraged to look closely at their subject, and then to look again even closer.
The teacher's role is to encourage each child to observe carefully and to record his findings. Mistakes in draughtsmanship and perspective are to be expected. These will be overcome as confidence grows. Initially, children would do well to make very simple line drawings and to ignore shading. If children are having trouble making something 'look right', the chances are that they are not seeing the shapes correctly. Discussion about the shapes in question will often solve the dilemma.

Evaluation: Do the drawings indicate that the subject has been closely observed?

Activity:	Developing drawings – individual painting.	
Concept:	Colour/texture/shape/ composition.	
Aim:	To develop the drawings done on location into a finished composition.	
	See Colour Plates P & Q	

Resources needed:
1. Sugar paper; newspaper; paints; palettes; water jars; paint rags; brushes; chalk; projector.
2. Sketches done on location.
3. Reproductions and slides of paintings of everyday scenes in which the artist has shown details of texture and surface, e.g. Stanley Spencer, Renoir, El Greco, Frans Hals, Vermeer, Velasquez.

Preparation:
Cut sugar paper to approximately 40 × 30 cm.
Cover tables with newspaper and give out painting materials.
Display the reproductions of paintings.

Introduction:
Refer to the reproductions on the wall and show slides. Discuss how the artists have composed their pictures. Which part do we look at first? Why? Can we tell the time of day by the light? Which colours appear most often in a painting? Which colours has the artist used for the brightly-lit areas and the shadows? How has the artist made us more aware of the surfaces, shapes and textures?
The purpose of this discussion is not to seek a formula for making paintings, but rather to make children aware of the different ways in which artists have portrayed everyday subjects.

Development:
Ask the children to compose a picture based on their sketches. Ideas should be lightly sketched in chalk and the following points should be considered:
1. Has the picture something in the foreground and the background?
2. What should the viewer notice first, place this just off the centre of the paper.
3. From which direction is the light coming?
Tell the children not to draw details with chalk. When the composition has been sketched in they should start painting. There are no rules about whether to paint the foreground first or last, but, generally speaking, it is probably advisable to start with the largest areas of colour, or those with not much detail, and try to get the balance of tones about right. Try to vary the tones so that the painting is not mostly dark or light colours. Think of the light colours balancing the dark. As the paintings progress, encourage the children to refer to their sketches, and to add details of texture and pattern to their paintings, ensuring that there are areas of contrast – light/dark, patterned/plain.

Evaluation:
Did the information from their sketches appear in their paintings?
Did the introduction evoke discussion?
Did the children's paintings indicate that they had been influenced by the reproductions?

Activity:	Developing drawings – working large.
Concept:	Colour/texture/shape/composition.
Aim:	To develop drawings done on location into a large scale composition. To consolidate previous work on composition and discuss the work of artists.

See Colour Plate O

Resources needed:
1. Projector; paints; palettes; water jars; paint rags; brushes; chalk; very large sheets of backing paper, frieze paper or a large blank wall surface in the corridor that may be painted.
2. Children's drawings of trees, bushes, animals, etc. Reproductions and slides of landscape paintings and murals.

Preparation:
Take the children out to draw and make notes of trees, bushes, animals, etc.
Display the reproductions of paintings.
Put newspaper on the floor in front of the surface to be painted. Ensure that the paint is thick and creamy.

Introduction:
Refer to the reproductions on the wall and show the slides. Discuss the work as indicated in the introduction of Session 107. Also refer to the scale of the paintings, particularly that of the murals.
Try to make the children aware of:
1. How artists have given the impression of distance.
2. How they have painted the subjects already sketched by the children.
3. The variety of greens and browns in a landscape.
4. The different treatments of the sky.

Development:
Suggest that the children work together on a large scale picture of an imaginary landscape, but based on things they have seen and drawn. This could be a park, wood, farm or a type of landscape inspired by one of the reproductions. Decide how many children could comfortably work on the wall at the same time, and ask for that number of volunteers to make a start. The remainder of the children could, perhaps paint individual landscapes.
The volunteers should map out the main composition lines with chalk, indicating the skyline and any other main features, e.g. a lake.
After referring to their own sketches, they should then decide whether to paint in something in the foreground, middle distance or background. The teacher's role at this point is crucial in helping children to decide on a suitable scale so that a child painting a cow in the foreground is aware of its size in relation to a sheep in the background and vice versa.
Children take it in turns to add to the picture, the whole class occasionally discussing its progress and making suggestions for additions and changes. The least confident children might be responsible for painting areas of grass and sky.

Evaluation:
Were the children able to transfer the information in their drawings to paintings of a different scale?
Did the introduction evoke discussion?
Was the influence of the reproductions evident in the children's work?

Activity: Developing drawings – group project.

Concept: Colour/texture/shape.

Aim: To develop the drawings done on location into a large scale composition.

See Colour Plate O

Resources needed:
1. Paints; palettes; water jars; paint rags; brushes; chalk; very large sheets of backing paper, frieze paper or a large blank wall surface in the corridor that may be painted.
2. Children's drawings of a particular area that is being studied.

Preparation: Take the children out to do drawings and make notes with a view to reproducing that area in the form of a large painting or collage. The teacher's task is to ensure that several children are not drawing the same thing. Each child might, for example, be responsible for one particular building in a row of buildings.
Put newspaper on the floor in front of the surface to be painted.
Ensure that the paint is thick and creamy.

Introduction: Discuss with the children the scale of the painting. In the case of the one illustrated, which was approximately 3×10 m, it was decided to draw a horizontal chalk line about half-way up. Everything below that line was the river and near bank. Everything above was what the children saw along the river front on the far bank. The size of the buildings was quickly decided upon and children started to enlarge their sketches on to sheets of rough paper.

Development: About a dozen volunteers started to paint directly on to the wall, working from original sketches. The boy who drew the house on the far left of the row was the first to paint it in. The girl who drew the house alongside, painted hers next and so on. Other children were busy painting in trees, ducks, rowing boats, water, etc. The beauty of a large project like this is that there are lots of fairly simple, menial tasks such as painting sky and water, which allow the less able to contribute and thereby build up their confidence.
When children sketch, details, such as the pattern work of bricks and railings, are often missed. If original sketches do not contain sufficient information children should, if possible, be encouraged to return and look again.

Evaluation: Did the children have sufficient information in their sketches to paint with confidence?
Were the children able to transfer the information in their drawings to paintings of a different scale?

Activity: Christmas mobiles.

Concept: Colour/form/balance.

Aim: To allow children practice at designing three-dimensional mobiles.
To consolidate previous work on colour.

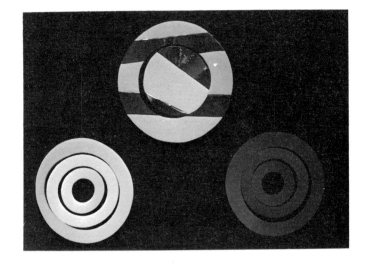

Resources needed:
1. Thin cardboard; scissors; pencils; cotton; PVA adhesive; galvanised wire; wire cutters or pliers; string; many circular objects for templates; sticky tape.
2. Photographs of mobiles by Calder, Martin, etc.

Preparation: Cut the card into pieces approximately 20 × 20 cm.
Give out circular shapes.

Introduction: Show the photographs of mobiles and explain that they are meant to be pieces of sculpture, but hanging in space and moving around slowly. They are designed to be seen from many different positions. This is an important point to remember when designing a mobile.

Development: The children are to design a mobile based on circles within circles that will move round by themselves, suspended from cotton. Children should start by cutting out the largest possible circle from their piece of card. Other circles should then be cut from within this first circle. Trim 5 mm from each of the smaller circles and place them, one within the other, as illustrated. Stick a piece of cotton in a straight line across all the circles. When dry, suspend the circles from a piece of galvanised wire so that they each spin independently. Make other groups of circles and suspend them from the same wire so that they balance. Hang the mobile from a central piece of string. After adjusting the position of the groups of circles so that they are equally balanced, tape the cotton to the wire so that it cannot move. Consider different ways of decorating the circles. Shiny papers will reflect the light from different angles as the circles move round. Circles could be painted with harmonious colours on one side and discordant on the other. Others might be painted with tints and shades of the same colour. Ask the children to consider how other groups of circles might be suspended that would fit in with the mobile and yet make it more interesting to look at.
These mobiles should blend with decorations suggested in Sessions 64, 79 and 111.

Evaluation: Was there a feeling of balance and unity to each of the mobiles?
Were some of the previous colour experiments evident in the results?

Activity: Decorations for Christmas.

Concept: Pattern/shape.

Aim: To allow children to practise paper sculpture.
To consolidate previous work on radial patterns.

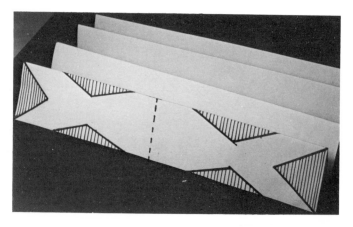

Resources needed: Any fairly stiff papers or card; scissors; pencils; rulers; stapler; cotton.

Preparation: Cut paper to approximately 60 × 40 cm.
Give out materials.

Introduction: Explain that the intention is to make three-dimensional stars using a simple paper sculpture technique.
1. Fold the paper in half to 30 × 40 cm. Repeat twice more to give seven creases.
2. Fold some of these creases the other way until you have a concertina effect.
3. Fold up the concertina until you have a strip. Fold the strip in half, crease, then open out again.
4. On one side of the strip draw, then cut out, shapes similar to those shaded in the illustration.
5. Pinching the outside strips, stretch the paper round into a star shape, then staple.

Development: After the initial experiment, it will be realised that the paper may be cut in a number of different ways to give a great variety of patterns.
The stars could then be suspended from cotton and made into mobiles as described in Session 110, or used as decoration in conjunction with the circular mobiles.
These stars should blend with decorations suggested in Sessions 64, 79, 110.

Evaluation: Did the children change and develop the ideas originally presented to them?
Were the radial designs symmetrical?

Activity: Fabric project – tie and dye.

Concept: Pattern/colour.

Aim: To consolidate previous work on tie and dye.

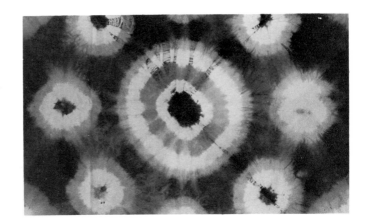

Resources needed:
1. Offcuts of white or light-coloured cotton material; string; Dylon cold water dye – two colours that will give an 'overprint' effect, e.g. Bahama Blue and Sahara Sun; Primrose and Coral; Emerald and Scarlet; rubber gloves; salt; soda; two buckets or large bowls; mixing spoons; newspaper.
2. Preferably examples of tie-dyed materials, or photographs showing the results of different ways of tieing.

Preparation: *Dye bucket:* dissolve two level teaspoonsful of dye in half a litre of warm water.
Fixative bucket: dissolve four tablespoonsful of common salt and one tablespoonful of household soda in half a litre of hot water.
Allow the solution in both buckets to cool, then mix both solutions together. Once mixed this dyebath is effective for a maximum of three hours. One dyebath needed per colour. Each child will need at least one piece of material approximately 15 × 15 cm, several pieces of string approximately 20 cm long and a sheet of newspaper. Tell the children to put their initials in biro in one corner of the material.

Introduction: Show the examples of tie and dye and suggest starting with the radial design in two colours. Children are advised to work in pairs. One takes a square of material about 15 × 15 cm and, holding the centre with thumb and finger of one hand, allows the rest of the material to fall in fairly even folds.
The partner wraps string tightly round the material and ties a double knot. More string is tied tightly round the material until about half the material is covered by string. It is then ready for the dyeing process:
1. Wet the material and squeeze out excess water.
2. Immerse the material in the dyebath made up with the lighter of the two colours.
3. Dye it for at least thirty minutes, stirring every ten minutes.
4. Lift it up with a stick and squeeze out surplus dye using rubber gloves.
5. Put it on to a sheet of newspaper and carry it to the sink or bucket of water. Rinse thoroughly, then squeeze out surplus water. Wash in warm, soapy water.

Development: Undo about half of the string and then retie it, but in slightly different places. The material is now ready to be dyed the second colour and the dyeing process explained above should be repeated: using a fresh dyebath.
There are many other simple, but effective, ways of producing designs. When children have experimented on small pieces of material, they might like to try dyeing items from home, e.g. handkerchiefs, towels, tea towels, flannels, cushion covers. In fact, almost any plain, light-coloured material could be patterned in this way.

Evaluation: Were evenly-spaced radial designs produced?
Did the children achieve designs with four colours, including white?

Activity: Fabric project – block printing.

Concept: Pattern/colour/shape/texture.

Aim: To consolidate previous work on pattern.
To teach how to cut a block for printing on to fabric.

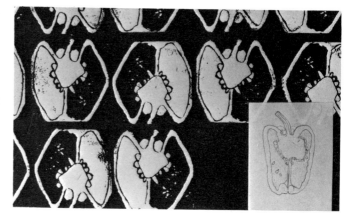

Resources needed: Thin pieces of foam rubber; jam jar lids; blocks of board or thick plywood up to 10×10 cm; PVA adhesive; card; carbon paper; mallet or hammer; fabric dyes; newspaper; scrap paper; clean offcuts of white cotton fabric; corks, sticky tape; sharp knives.
For notes on dyes see page 157.

Preparation: Cut the foam rubber to fit the jam jar lids.

Introduction: Demonstrate how to make a simple block print that repeats to form a pattern.
1. Cut the top 5 mm of a cork into a square, rectangle or triangle.
2. Put some fabric dye into the foam pad and make sure that it soaks in.
3. Press the cork on to the pad and print on to some scrap paper. Repeat the process so that you have a line of identical prints from the cork.
4. Do other lines, but this time vary the arrangements. Refer to Session 81 for ideas.

Development: When children have practised with corks and other suitable printing blocks on paper, they are then ready to print on to fabric.
1. Make an even pad of six pieces of newspaper, cut 2 cm smaller all round than the piece of fabric.
2. Pin or stick with tape the fabric to a firm base, with the newspaper pad under the fabric. Print.
After a few experiments with colours and textures, the children could embark on a project designing and printing table mats, table cloths, aprons, oven gloves, ties, etc.
There are many ways of making blocks for printing. The illustration shows how a drawing has been developed into a block made from cardboard.
1. The drawing is traced on to thin cardboard.
2. This is cut out and stuck on to a block of wood or thick plywood.
3. When dry, the card block is pressed into the dye, as described above, put on to the fabric and the back of the block is hammered gently.

Evaluation: Did the children demonstrate that they could make repeat prints?
Was the fabric printed evenly and neatly, or was it messy and the pattern untidy?
Were the children keen to extend the ideas presented to them?

Activity:	Fabric project – transfer printing.
Concept:	Colour/shape/texture/pattern.
Aim:	To consolidate previous work on pattern and symmetry. To teach the process of transfer printing on to fabric.

See Colour Plate A

Resources needed:	1. Duplicating paper; scissors; Fabricrayons – see page 158; electric iron; newspaper.
	2. Pictures and actual examples of radiating designs in nature, e.g. daisy, dandelion.
	3. Synthetic material – offcuts of Crimplene or nylon.
Preparation:	Display the experiments done during Session 113.
	Ask children to bring in any natural examples of radiating designs.
	Cut the material into pieces approximately 20 × 30 cm.
	Cut the paper to approximately 20 × 20 cm.
Introduction:	Refer to the work on display and praise good examples of craftsmanship and design.
	Discuss the examples of radiating design and re-cap briefly on symmetrical patterns.
	Ask the children to choose one of the radiating designs as the basis for their fabric transfer print, and to draw it so that it almost fills the duplicating paper. Use any of the Fabricrayons and overlap the colours so that there is a heavy layer of crayon.
	For extra interest, rubbings from textured surfaces may be cut out and stuck to the drawing. When complete, cut away the background.
Development:	To transfer the drawing to the fabric:
	1. Spread the fabric out on to a pad of several sheets of newspaper.
	2. Place the drawing *face down* on to the fabric.
	3. Cover the drawing and fabric with a clean sheet of paper but *not* newsprint.
	4. Press with a hot iron for at least a minute, ensuring that the iron is kept moving and that the material does not scorch.
	5. Hold down one side of the drawing while lifting the other to see if the drawing has transferred on to the fabric. If it has not, continue ironing. No further fixing is required.
	After several experiments with colours on small pieces of material, children might like to decorate the edges of garments made of synthetic material and then go on to decorating T-shirts, blouses, dresses, etc.
Evaluation:	Were the children able to interpret their natural radial patterns?
	Were the children keen to experiment and develop ideas?

Activity:	Fabric project – appliqué.
Concept:	Colour/shape/texture.
Aim:	To encourage children to study an object and interpret it in terms of appliqué; to increase powers of observation and allow experimentation with fabrics.

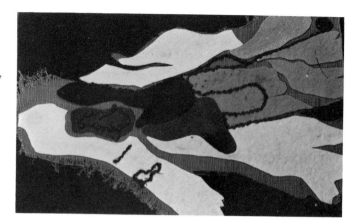

Resources needed:

1. Fabric scraps sorted according to colour; string; threads; plain material approximately 40 × 30 cm; thick card or hardboard approximately 30 × 20 cm; fabric glue; needles and cottons; scissors and pins; scraps of white and coloured paper; pencils.
2. Natural objects with fairly simple shapes.
3. Actual examples or photographs of fabric appliqué.

Preparation: Ask the children to bring objects that they would like to work from, and materials that might be useful for their appliqué.

Introduction: Show children the examples of appliqué and discuss the techniques used.
Explain that their appliqués will be tackled in three stages:

1. *Shape.* The main shapes should be cut out of paper and placed on to the backing board. The shapes should not be drawn first – use the scissors as a pencil. Shapes may be overlapped, and if they don't fit straight away, try again with more paper. The design should fill the area.
2. *Colour.* Decide on a colour scheme, then choose a background colour from the plain material, and about three other pieces of material for the shapes. Consider contrast of tone.
3. *Texture.* If the object has textural interest, choose threads, strings, beads, etc., that will express the right quality.

Development: When the main shapes have been cut from paper, use them as a template to cut out the shapes from material. These may be sewn and/or stuck into position on the backing material. Then additional material, string, threads, beads, etc., may be added for textural interest. When the design is complete, the backing material should be stretched around the backing board, and stuck down on the reverse side.

Evaluation: Did the results indicate that the children had chosen appropriate shapes, colours and ways of texturing their design?
Were the designs visually interesting?
Was there evidence of experimentation?

Activity: Studying an artist.

Concept: Appreciation of art. Colour/ shape/texture/tone/ composition.

Aim: To encourage children to study in depth the work of a particular artist.

See Colour Plate B

Resources needed:
1. Painting materials; rulers; tracing paper; pencils.
2. As much material as can be collected on the work of famous artists. It is advisable to start collecting well beforehand. The library and county resources centre should be approached first. Local schools of art may be willing to lend material and also the secondary schools in the vicinity. Parents, too, may be willing to lend books.

Preparation: Ensure that each child has one good colour reproduction to work from.

Introduction: Ask the children to choose a colour reproduction that appeals to them. Explain that they will be expected to:
1. Find out about the artist and make a folder to contain what has been found out. This could include writing and sketches of some of his other work.
2. Make a copy of the chosen reproduction.
3. Write a critical appraisal of the reproduction – a complete description for, say, a blind person.

Development: The order in which the above tasks are carried out is not crucial. It might be useful to demonstrate the squaring-up method of copying the reproduction. The main shapes of the composition are traced on to tracing paper. This is covered in squares of, say, 1 cm. The same number of squares are drawn on to a large sheet of painting paper, but enlarged so that they just fit on to the paper. The children then have a guide for enlarging their drawing from the tracing paper to the large sheet. Tell them to lightly sketch only the main shapes of the reproduction, with no detail, then to make a painted copy of the reproduction, matching the colours and details as carefully as possible. Display the reproduction with their copies and let the children make a verbal report on their findings.

Evaluation: Did the children develop an interest in their artist and enjoy discovering things about him/ her?
Did the written appraisals indicate an enquiring and perceptive attitude?
Were there any unexpected outcomes?

Activity: Studying an artist – Vincent
                       Van Gogh.

Concept: Colour.

Aim: To help children to appreciate
                       the work of Van Gogh through
                       critical appraisal.

                       See Colour Plate D

> **Starry Night by Van Gogh.**
>
> The thing that hits me most is the emotion he puts into this picture. It is about a village underneath a disturbed sky. The whirls in the sky make it a bit brighter, in some of the whirls the stars and moon show up the oil paint dabs and the colours. The main whirl comes barging into the picture like a thunderstorm. The hills roll gently under the turmoil and the bushes roll into the village. The village has all its reddish-yellow lamps on and the church stands alone, forlorne and black. The great cypress tree gets the picture going by looking like witches hands looking green and old.
>
> I think its a very nice picture because I like the way he puts emotions on canvas. Also I like the feel of trouble in his mind. He must have liked gloomy colours because he put greens, browns, blacks and greys but I am not sure because he then puts whites, yellows, oranges and reds in the sky.
>
> Susanne Guy

Resources   A slide and print of *Starry Night* by Van Gogh; projector; a print of any other painting by
needed: another artist; pen and writing paper.

Preparation: Set up projector.

Introduction: Show the print of a painting by an artist other than Van Gogh. Ask the children what they
                       think of it. Do they like or dislike it – why? Is it happy or sad? How can you tell? Can you tell
                       anything about the artist from the way it was painted? Continue to discuss the painting until
                       you feel that the children have had their eyes opened to several different aspects of the
                       painting.
                       Explain how certain artists can paint a picture of a quite ordinary scene in a very personal
                       way. Sometimes the picture will convey a mood or feeling and we might even be able to
                       discover something about the artist if we look carefully enough.

Development: With the exception of just two children, ask the class to close their eyes. Project the slide of
                       Starry Night and ask the first child to describe the picture as carefully as possible, but without
                       referring to the colours. Then ask the second child to add to this description, but referring
                       particularly to the colours used and *how* this picture has been painted.
                       Tell the children to open their eyes. Explain that the picture was painted about 100 years ago
                       by Van Gogh, a man who was sometimes very happy, but who could also be extremely sad.
                       We can usually tell whether he was happy or sad by the colours he used and the way in which
                       he painted. Don't invite verbal opinions at this stage, otherwise the children might simply
                       copy one another. Ask them to write down as much as they can about the picture, including a
                       description for a blind man, their opinion of the picture and their opinion of the artist.

Evaluation: Did the pieces of writing suggest that the children had looked closely at the painting?
                       Were the children able to offer an opinion about the painting and the artist?

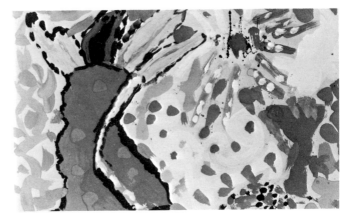

Activity:	Interpreting prose.
Concept:	Colour/tone.
Aim:	To encourage children to use paint expressively. To consolidate the experiences of Session 117.

Resources needed:

1. Newspaper; any paper; chalk; water jars, one between two; paint rags, one each; brushes; paints.
2. Poems or stories that describe violent motion in the air such as *The Trillions* by Nicholas Fisk.
   Any lively music, e.g. *Night on a Bare Mountain* by Mussorgsky.

Preparation: Display results of the previous two sessions with a print of *Starry Night*.

Introduction: Read out some of the critical appraisals written during the previous session, and remind children of the method employed by Van Gogh to suggest movement.
Next read any descriptive passages that strongly suggest violent motion in the air.
Ask the children to choose just one of the passages, and to make a painting that expresses the feeling of movement through the air. The painting does not need to be photographic or realistic, as the chief aim is to use colours and brush strokes to create dynamic effects.

Development: As most of the movement will take place in the sky, tell children to draw an horizon in chalk low down on their paper, then to paint directly without previous drawing. In order to create the right sort of atmosphere, it might be useful to have some lively background music playing while the children are working.

Evaluation: Did the paintings express the feeling of movement?
Were there any unusual outcomes?

Activity:	Clay project I.
Concept:	Form/texture.
Aim:	To teach children how to make decorative clay beads.

Resources needed:	Clay; galvanised wire; builder's sand; newspaper; any mark-making tools, e.g. lolly sticks, nails, twigs, screws, etc.; cocktail sticks; blunt table knives.
Preparation:	Cover tables with newspaper. Each child will need approximately ¼ kilo of clay, about two teaspoonsful of sand, about 30 cm of wire and a cocktail stick.
Introduction:	Tell the children to make a pancake with their clay and to knead in the sand as evenly as possible. Explain that an 'open-bodied' or gritty clay is needed because of the process of firing that will be employed. Demonstrate how to make a variety of bead shapes by: 1. Rolling clay into balls and ovoids. 2. Rolling out worms about 1 cm thick and chopping them up. 3. Pressing the worms into cuboids. Demonstrate how to texture the beads by gently pressing any of the mark-making tools into them.
Development:	Tell the children to curve their wire into a circle. When the beads are finished, they should be pierced with a cocktail stick to make a hole slightly bigger than the diameter of the wire. The beads should then be threaded on to the wire ready for firing. As clay shrinks slightly when it is fired, ensure that the wire is not fitted tightly into the bead, otherwise breakages will occur. The clay should dry out slowly, and be thoroughly dry before firing takes place. This could take at least a day, but it is advisable to make some test beads which are cracked open. If the inside of the clay is slightly darker than the outside, then it has not finished drying and should be left.
Evaluation:	Were the children able to make a variety of forms, and to texture them? Did the children appear to consider which forms should go together and in which order, or was the order purely arbitrary?

Activity: Clay project II – sawdust kiln.

Concept: Transforming the clay into pottery.

Aim: To teach children how to fire pottery in a sawdust kiln.

Resources needed: An old dustbin or five gallon metal oil drum; three house bricks; large sack of *dry* sawdust; newspaper; kindling sticks; matches; large nail and hammer.

Preparation: Pierce the metal drum or dustbin with a large nail and hammer. Make holes round the side and on the bottom about 15 cm apart. Arrange the bricks lying flat and in a triangular formation and stand the bin on them. Put about 10 cm of sawdust in the bottom of the bin.

Introduction: Show the children how to load the kiln by demonstrating with the first layer. Place the largest circle of wire-strung beads flat on to the layer of sawdust. Ensure that the beads are at least 5 cm from the edge of the kiln. If there is room for a smaller circle of beads inside this one, with a gap of least 5 cm between them, then place one in. Cover the beads with about 10 cm of sawdust.
Tell the children to load successive layers in exactly the same way until the kiln is full or all of the beads are loaded in. Try to finish up with about 15 cm of sawdust.

Development: The kiln should preferably be lit first thing in the morning. Build a small fire on the top of the sawdust, using the newspaper and kindling wood. When the flames have subsided and the sawdust is smoking nicely, put either a dustbin lid or sheet of asbestos on top to keep out any rain. For the first two hours the kiln should be topped up with sawdust to its original level about every half hour. After that, every hour or so should be sufficient. Ideally, the sawdust level should remain constant throughout the day, and when the time comes to leave the kiln to burn overnight, the sawdust should be at its original level. The kiln should then be left to completely burn itself out.
Depending on the strength and direction of the wind, the kiln might take forty-eight hours to completely burn through. Wait until the beads have cooled sufficiently to take them out by hand.
They may then be polished with furniture or boot polish, or varnished if a high gloss finish is required.

Evaluation: Did the children enjoy this Session?
Did the children load the kiln properly and keep it topped up?
Did the kiln go out, if so, why?
Was the fired clay really hard, or brittle and soft?

Questions commonly asked by teachers

Isn't an art scheme likely to inhibit free expression?

Teachers bitten by the free expression bug have allowed children to meander from one activity to the next with scant regard to the careful acquisition of skills and the discipline necessary for true free expression. For example, for children with little or no real understanding of how to organise colour, being asked to express a subject in paint must be rather like an adult being tossed a phrase book in an unknown language and being told to express himself in that language. Even the youngest child can make daubs on paper and, at a certain stage in his education, this may be considered to be educationally valid, but in order that children might be able to express ideas, inner feelings or emotions through paint, they must first be taught the language of colour, which is just part of the language of the artist.

It is reasonable to expect that children will acquire certain basic skills by the age of about eleven, which can be developed by the art specialist later on. Skill should be developed systematically, though, and teachers should be conscious of their role in developing particular concepts at a particular stage. It is important, therefore, that there is staff liaison so that teachers are aware of one another's schemes of work and can build with confidence on to what has gone before.

Teaching art can be compared with teaching someone to drive a car. Initially the instructor explains a few basic principles and lets the driver try them out. The next lesson consolidates what was learned previously, with perhaps a few more techniques added. By overlapping skills learned from one lesson to the next, the driver slowly builds up the confidence as well as acquiring mastery, the transference of skills and concepts from one lesson to the next being of prime importance.

How should art be taught in primary schools?

Primary schools seem to fit into one of two categories. Those that appreciate the value of a well-organised art scheme and can point to positive benefits derived in other subject areas such as language, mathematics and science; secondly, those that regard art as a frill to be dispensed with when more important matters arise.

Until teachers become convinced that art has a unique contribution to make, it will remain the Cinderella subject along with all the other so-called non-essential subjects.

Teachers of young children have usually had only a brief training in how to teach art, and an even briefer one in the practice of art, yet almost without exception they are obliged to teach art. Some thoroughly enjoy the challenge, some dread each art lesson and the majority survive from week to week on new ideas and tips gleaned from magazines, the television, after-school refresher courses and one another.

In spite of the lack of formal training, many do a fine job of teaching art, but sadly, because of general lack of cohesion in teaching the subject at primary level, much good art teaching is ignored or not taken into account by teachers at later stages in the education system. Why should the middle or high school art teacher largely disregard the efforts of colleagues in the primary school, and assume that primary children have done no art at all? One answer could be that in most areas in the country there is little or no follow-through in art from primary to subsequent stages, yet this is not the case in those subjects that have fairly clearly defined goals, and where primary schools are seen to be underpinning the work of the next stage.

In mathematics and language, for example, everyone is aware that the role of the primary teacher is to provide children with basic skills upon which secondary teachers can build an educational programme. The success of the operation is aided by the use of record cards and reports which are handed from teacher to teacher and, sometimes, from school to school. Although methods vary tremendously, primary schools are highly successful in carrying out the task and secondary schools can confidently predict attainment levels of incoming pupils in those two subjects, from which the basis of their curriculum is formed.

The general expectation of the specialist art teacher, however, is quite different. He usually assumes, and not always correctly, that his new pupils have had little or no proper art instruction upon which he can base his curriculum. It is quite usual for children taking art at their new school to be set tasks which are either so familiar as to appear tedious, or which seem to bear no relation to their conception of art as conveyed by their primary teacher. It is not surprising that most children quickly lose interest in art at around the age of eleven or twelve.

Art educators have strongly argued that it would be inappropriate to provide teachers with a common syllabus for art, fearing that schools would return to the rigid, sterile approach towards art teaching that was witnessed at the turn of the century. However, there appears to be a concensus of opinion that there are many broad bands of experience that teachers of art at every level of the educational system should be aware of, and which can contribute towards the art education of their children.

These broad areas of experience can be defined and broken down into units of learning or lessons that would be suitable for a particular class.

What role should art play in the primary school?

In primary schools art and craft tends to have two roles. Firstly, it is used in conjunction with other subjects for project or topic work. Art might play a major role when learning revolves around a particular craft, such as weaving. More usually, however, it is used simply as a back-up for the project with children illustrating folders or painting friezes on a given theme. In schools where art and craft is used *only* in this way, it is quite possible that art education is likely to be incomplete or, at best, fragmented. A child might spend most of the afternoon painting his model fire engine red, but at the end will have no more understanding of colour than when he started. In other words, that experience will have added little to his art education, but in the teacher's mind he has been 'doing art', because he has been using materials normally associated with art. It is not suggested that art has no part to play and should not be used in this connection, but it should be appreciated that visual and aesthetic awareness is unlikely to be one of the outcomes. For this to take place, a carefully considered series of lessons must also be included alongside the project work.

Secondly, art is also used as an educational tool in its own right, adding an ingredient to the curriculum that is unique to art. In this instance lessons are provided which aim to teach children fundamental principles of art. On an average throughout the year, infants may have one lesson each week, and juniors one about every two or three weeks. This will vary from school to school and much will depend on how art is used in conjunction with project work. The scheme outlined in this book is just one example of how fundamental principles could be introduced at different stages.

What should we be aiming for?

It would be helpful if teachers could find a common goal, or goals for teaching art. I think most teachers would agree that it is unlikely that many, if any, of their children will earn a living through art, and there seems to be little point in trying to prepare the whole class towards that end. Without denying for a moment the value of experiencing practical activities in art and craft, perhaps it would be worth asking ourselves what our main aims might be, and how we might achieve those aims.

There appears to be some confusion in the minds of many primary teachers on these points. I once asked a group of primary teachers at the beginning of an In-Service course to write down their main reason for teaching art, and the following answers are fairly typical of the replies I received:

'Children like doing it.'

'It allows children to express themselves.'
'Because I have to.'
'It teaches manual dexterity.'

None of the answers are wrong, but none of them could be described as good educational reasons for including art and craft in a curriculum which aims to prepare children for our technological society.

If we were to put a similar question to a teacher of language in the primary school, her simple answer would probably be 'to enable the children to become literate'. A teacher of maths might reply 'to enable the children to become numerate', and it is likely that their specialist counterparts in the secondary school would not be unhappy with those general aims. I doubt if the specialist art teachers would be as pleased with the replies given by my in-service group. The art teacher's simplistic reply to the question would probably be 'to enable children to become visually and aesthetically aware'. But it is unlikely that many primary teachers would have put this as the main purpose of their art lessons, and some would be uncertain how to achieve it. This could be at the root of the problem of linking the two camps.

What is meant by visually and aesthetically aware?

At the primary level we should be introducing children to visual and tactile qualities to be found all around us. Children at this age seem to have a natural curiosity that we should foster and develop. As their perception of the immediate environment increases, so will their capacity to react to works of art.

But aesthetic awareness does not apply only to looking at pictures in an art gallery. The teacher who makes a conscious effort to provide a meaningful visual education will be preparing the ground for children's future with works of art, architecture and many aspects of design.

Unless the child's perception of colour, line, shape, form, texture, tone and pattern is fully developed he cannot properly appreciate the influences that shape man's mode of thinking and feeling. Conversely, children who have some understanding of these elements of art will find it easier to react to and discuss works of art, and this will usually generate interest and provide encouragement to their own creative efforts. At each stage of a child's development from the nursery school onwards, aesthetic awareness should be considered an important part of their education. The child who has learned how to investigate his surroundings, how to organise his experiences into some kind of pattern and how to start to hypothesise, has the best start in all aspects of later learning, not only in art.

141

Which activities are likely to enable children to become aesthetically aware?

Art in schools usually involves children doing or making something so that the end product might be a picture or model. Most art educators would thoroughly endorse the notion that it is desirable to encourage children to give visible form to their inner visions. Making art is important, of course, but there are other aspects of art education that are also important, and these have been largely ignored.

For various reasons, the historical and cultural aspects of art have been sadly neglected by primary teachers, and it has been assumed that if children were allowed simply to make their own art they would, as a consequence, learn to appreciate and discuss other works of art. This is not the case. In order that children shall be able to fully appreciate those forms that we call works of art, attention and time must be given to build up critical skills as well as practical skills. This can be done by studying art of the past, using specific aesthetic frames of reference and asking children to talk and write about it, as well as make drawings from it.

This does not imply that the primary teacher should be expected to teach the history of art, but she has an important role to play in helping children appreciate their own culture and that of other people.

The key to appreciation is observation

The more a child is encouraged to really look at, touch and talk about the things he is going to draw, the more detailed his work will be.

This is where the teacher is needed, not to interfere with the child's drawing, but rather to ask relevant and searching questions so that the child looks again and notices more. Whether the child is looking at petals on a flower, the carving on a piece of furniture, a picture by Constable or the stained-glass windows in a church, the teacher's questions about colour, texture, pattern, etc., will increase the child's perception of such qualities and, in turn, his aesthetic awareness.

Children could, for example, start to analyse the colours used by a particular artist, and this information might then be transferred to their own creative efforts.

Which broad areas of experience would be appropriate at each level of learning?

The problem for many primary teachers is that their own level of understanding about basic art elements such as colour and line is limited, and therefore they feel at a loss to develop an area of learning in which they lack confidence. This need not be the case though, and one of the aims of the Session outlines in this book is to systematically introduce to the *teacher* as well as the children, an approach to studying the basic art elements which make up the language of art.

Primary teachers introduce children to the language of mathematics and English upon which the secondary teacher builds. In the same way it seems reasonable that primary teachers should introduce children to the language of art. If all primary children received similar broad areas of experience that resulted in greater comprehension of the language of art, teachers at later stages could develop curricula that took this into account. See notes on the language of art, page 145.

How much time will a proper art scheme take?

The initial reaction might be that the timetable is too crowded already and time is simply not available for *more* art. The suggestion is not necessarily to allow more time for art at the expense of other subjects, but to use whatever time is available to reach for a common goal. It is my belief that many activities are carried out in schools under the banner of art and craft which do virtually nothing to increase children's powers of perception or understanding of artistic concepts – the main aim in some cases seems to be to allow children to play around with a great variety of materials and to produce cheerful-looking work with which to decorate the corridors. Consideration is rarely given to what children have learned and whether the time could have been spent more profitably.

The plea, therefore, is not for more time, but rather that primary teachers should raise their educational sights when planning art and craft activities.

How much money will this take?

Another quite understandable concern is that a properly-structured curriculum in art and craft is bound to be expensive. Once again, this is not necessarily the case, and indeed there is merit in taking a careful look at the art materials that have traditionally been used in the school and asking whether or not they are educationally relevant or necessary. In recent years considerable pressure has been applied by manufacturers of art materials and some publishers to make teachers feel that good art teaching is synonymous with a great variety of materials, and that slick, easy results are preferable to the careful, and sometimes laborious acquisition of skill. Without doubt, children enjoy producing results that others admire, and part of the teacher's task is to smooth out problems on the road to success, but this should not necessarily lead to sterile or gimmicky lessons where the end result is prescribed. This is often the case. There can be little artistic merit attached to a lesson in which every child in the class produces an identical result, yet one sees this happening time and again, and in the name of art and craft.

Conversely, I am constantly amazed at the powers of concentration of even very young children who have been encouraged to observe closely and record their findings through drawing. I have watched children of five or six years old patiently studying natural forms in the classroom and then spending as long as *three hours* on one drawing, without any pressure from the teacher. This does not correspond with the conviction of most infant teachers that small children are unable to concentrate for long periods. Purely from the economic point of view, a child engaged in doing a pencil drawing for three hours uses far fewer materials than one engaged in several diverse activities over the same period!

Naturally, if art and craft is to be taught properly, a range of art materials must be provided and time must be allowed, but a carefully-planned programme of art and craft is likely to produce more worthwhile results and make the best possible use of the resources available, than one that relies heavily on stimulating children's interest with a series of novelty lessons that require a wide assortment of materials.

At the end of this book on page 153 a list of all the materials needed to implement the 120 Sessions outlined, is included. In most cases schools will already have these materials in stock.

The language of art

We are all brought up with the knowledge that words are the individual elements of our language, and that by putting words together we are able to express ideas, emotions and what we see and know.

We also refer to the language of art, and the language of music and mathematics.

The individual elements of the language of art are **line, colour, tone, texture, form, pattern** and **shape**.

If we seriously intend to provide children with a proper basic education in art and craft, these elements must be understood. There is no need to teach them separately, but at each of the six stages there should be a conscious effort to discuss and allow practice in each of these elements.

Line

Line is the element most used in drawing and, though what is being drawn rarely has a line round it, the funny thing is that the subject is usually easily recognisable from a line drawing. Even a very young child can symbolise with line, and does so effortlessly.

Initially, children should receive plenty of encouragement to experiment with different line-making tools like chalk, crayon, pencil, ball-point and felt-tip pens and twigs dipped into paint. Discussion about the lines that children make will throw up adjectives that describe the quality of their lines – wiggly, dotty, jumpy, curly, rough, thick, thin, etc. This, in turn, should help them to consider the appropriate drawing medium for particular subjects, e.g. chalk might be fine for drawing a fluffy chick but a ball-point pen might be better for drawing all the lines on the palm of your hand.

The stimulus or starting point for line work could be almost anything that is linear in character. Natural objects such as a tree root or the grain in wood lend themselves to a linear treatment. Children's natural fascination with detailed, imaginative subjects, such as battle scenes, could also provide impetus for experiments with line.

As an alternative to making marks on to paper, linear designs in relief could be made with string, drinking straws, thread stuck on to card, etc.

Colour

Initially children respond to colour purely for the pleasure it gives, and discussion should be concerned with naming colours and marks that children produce.

As infant paintings become more controlled and symbols appear, simple experiments in colour mixing should be encouraged. Displays of objects that are predominantly one colour could be the starting point for mixing and matching colours, which might lead on to paintings of only one colour. By closely observing the colours in natural forms and discussing them, children will build up a vocabulary of colour and appreciate that there are many different greens, blues, browns, etc.

Teachers should be prepared to apply basic colour theory, so that children's knowledge of colour is not left to chance.

When ordering paints it is not necessary to choose a vast range and children learn more about colour theory if they are forced to mix the colours that they need. The following is a guide to the basic range needed.

Start with black, white and the primary colours (yellow, red, blue). In theory you should be able to mix any other colour you need from these. In practice though, you'll need two of each of the primary colours – one *warm*, one *cool*.

Yellow $\begin{cases} \text{yellow ochre – a cool yellow} \\ \text{chrome yellow – a warm yellow.} \end{cases}$

Red $\begin{cases} \text{crimson – a cool red} \\ \text{vermillion or scarlet – a warm red.} \end{cases}$

Blue $\begin{cases} \text{cobalt – a cool blue} \\ \text{ultramarine – a warm blue.} \end{cases}$

Most colours can be mixed from these, but it is difficult to achieve a good turquoise and indian red (rich earth colour), so these might be ordered separately. Remember to order three times as much white as any other colour.

Tone

This is a way of referring to the lightness or darkness of colours.

When teachers are discussing colour they might ask 'Of these three blue pieces of paper, which is the darkest? Which is the lightest?' Or 'John has three different reds in his painting. Which is the lightest? Which is the darkest?'

The next step is to point out that not only does blue have different tonal values but that tonal differences exist between colours, e.g. crimson is darker than chrome yellow.

After practice and discussion, children will be able to distinguish between the tones of colours whose tonal values are close together. In much the same way as they are learning to sing in tune, so they will learn to sort out the right order of the 'notes' in colour, so as not to produce a jumble, or conversely, a flat, uninteresting effect.

In order to help children understand the different tonal values of quite different colours, tell them to imagine that a black and white photograph has been taken of them. Which would come out darkest and lightest on the photograph?

Texture

In artistic terms, texture implies something three-dimensional that owes its identity to touch as much as sight.

Outside school, young children are often ordered 'Not to touch!' But it is only through holding, feeling, picking and poking at surfaces that they gain a true understanding of what texture really means.

Teachers often invent texture games, where objects with interesting surfaces are put into a feelie-bag or box with a hole at the top just big enough for a child's hand. Words are invited to describe the surface of the object.

Other activities might include texture rubbing or making impressions of textures by pressing them with Plasticine.

When children understand the meaning of texture, they should be encouraged to explore the textural qualities of art materials. They will discover that they can invent their own textures, as well as recreate the appearance of real textures with pencils, pen and ink, paint, charcoal or a combination of them.

Pattern

The lives of children and adults alike are governed by pattern – the rising and setting of the sun, getting up, eating, going to bed – life is a series of repeated experiences.

Schools run to a similar routine each day and provide a rhythm to children's lives which they find comforting. It is this repetition that provides the pattern of life.

When explaining the term pattern to children, it is the repeating element that is important, even though adults often use the term loosely to describe practically any accidental or random arrangement of shapes or colours.

We can find endless examples of natural patterns around us, where shapes or colours are repeated, usually for purely functional rather than decorative reasons. In the animal kingdom pattern may be used to attract or camouflage, and one has only to slice an orange in half to find the most fascinating repetition of shapes.

Man-made patterns exist on brick walls, roofs, the windows on a block of flats, and so on.

The concept of pattern is built up in young children by letting them make their own. Anything plentiful could be used, such as leaves, matchsticks, seeds, pebbles, etc. They could be played about with initially and stuck down on to a piece of paper. The natural extension of this is printing patterns from fingers, corks, cotton reels and the like, first of all on paper and, at a later stage, on to fabric to produce both decorative and functional designs.

Shape

As previously stated, when shapes are drawn they are often described with lines, even though a line around the shape doesn't exist. In fact, the subject being drawn is probably a mass of different shapes all butting up to one another like a jigsaw puzzle.

When children look at things with a view to drawing them, they tend not to see this relationship of shapes, so it is the task of the teacher to make them aware, not only of the shapes that make up their subject, but also of the shapes that one sees around it. Try putting a white square in the middle of a black piece of paper and asking children what shapes they see. Move the square around so that different background shapes are made.

This could be taken a stage further. Put a plant with large regular-shaped leaves (cheese plant or rubber plant) against a white background and ask the children to draw the white shapes that they see behind the plant with white chalk on black paper, so that they end up with a silhouette in black of the plant.

At infant level, there should be plenty of discussion about shapes in the immediate environment. Some of them could be cut out of paper and folders of shapes could be made and added to.

The idea of proportion can be implanted by asking children to describe shapes in terms of width to length. Older children could be introduced to proportion through measurement drawing (Session 87).

Form

In simple terms, this is the element of art language that most concerns the sculptor. When he is making shapes from clay or stone, he thinks of those shapes occupying a space, and expects people to walk all round his forms and to look at them from every angle. They might be smooth, textured or even painted, but our understanding of the forms will be increased by handling them.

Children's understanding of form, therefore, is developed by handling a great variety of forms, and discussing them. When children go to the seaside they love to collect pebbles that have interesting shapes and textures, and this sort of activity could be developed in the classroom, perhaps making their own pebble shapes from clay or block salt, then discussing why they find certain forms pleasing.

Forms can be built up by an additive process, e.g. cardboard boxes stuck together or a wire frame with papier mâché added to it; or achieved by breaking down a solid mass, i.e. carving a block of polystyrene.

Form can also be suggested in a drawing or a painting by studying the way that light falls on to a solid object, then interpreting this on paper.

This sort of exercise is obviously dependent on an understanding of tonal relationships.

Display

Primary children tend to be most influenced by their visual experiences. Therefore teachers create a variety of environments some of which might encourage children to look more carefully at something. Others might stimulate their curiosity or imagination; this could be in preparation for a topic or school trip, or simply to cross-fertilise ideas between classes.

Putting children's work on display can help to foster a feeling of pride and achievement, and may also provide visitors to the school with an insight into the scope, validity and significance of children's work.

Items most usually found on display in schools tend to fall into three groups:

1. Plants and natural forms grouped by a teacher, in order to enhance the entrance to the school, or just to brighten up a dull part of the building.

2. Writing, paintings, drawings and craftwork done by the children but usually displayed by the teacher.

3. Collection of objects and photographs dealing with a particular topic, e.g. Victoriana. These may be collected by the children and the teacher.

Views differ markedly about what makes for a good display, and much depends on personal taste. Some people like neutral backings so that the work itself has maximum impact, while others start with brightly coloured backing sheets that have an eye-catching effect. Most successful displays, however, follow similar basic rules:

1. Aim for clarity and simplicity.

2. Do not put too much on display at the same time. Allow each piece room to breathe.

3. Design the display so that it looks as if items were meant for a particular area or space. Pictures pinned to the bottom of a display board so that they hang out of it will always look like afterthoughts, and make the display appear sloppy.

4. Any flat work, like writing or drawings, will be greatly enhanced by mounting.

5. Headings should be legible but not obtrusive.

Let us further consider points 3, 4 and 5.

Designing the display

Displays in schools may be mounted on display pin board, bare walls, windows, doors and cupboards. Whatever the size or type of surface, the basic rules apply.

Let us start with the most difficult display situation that exists in many of our older schools, where there are no display boards at all, and precious little wall space for any. Probably the cheapest and most versatile answer to this sort of problem is large rolls of corrugated paper. They are about two metres high and come in a variety of attractive colours. These could be cut up and tacked to disused doors, cupboards, partitions, etc. Alternatively they may be used as a free standing backcloth in a corridor or even a toilet area. They are particularly useful, though, for open days or when large displays are being mounted in the school hall. The best method for hanging work to corrugated card is to use dressmaking pins pushed almost vertically into the corrugations.

Before pinning work up it is advisable to spread it out on the floor, marked out to the same size as the display area. Work can then be shuffled about until a pleasing arrangement has been arrived at. It should be pinned up in the same corresponding positions with just two pins and, after minor adjustments, all four corners pinned or stapled. Do not overcrowd the display.

Any display will look more unified if the work is arranged so that some horizontal and vertical edges are aligned. This applies also to the headings.

Mounting

Even the most insignificant-looking piece of writing or drawing can be transformed with a mount round it. That is not to say it will improve the quality of the work, but may significantly boost the confidence of the child who did it, who may, as a result, improve the quality of his next piece of work.

Mounting need not be an expensive, time-consuming business either. In most cases the mounting paper should be cut to about 1 cm larger all round than the piece of work being mounted. If dressmaking pins are used in the corners of the piece of work, both the work and mount will be attached to the wall together, thus making it unnecessary to stick the two together. At the end of the display the mounting paper may then be re-used.

Double mounts are particularly impressive for paintings. Colours should be chosen carefully to enhance the colours in the painting. The outer margin should be slightly wider than the inner one. Bottom margins should be slightly wider than top ones.

Headings

Some displays will need a title or several captions. The main title should be placed off-centre but not too near the edge of the display area. If sub-headings are also used, they should be smaller than the main title.

All headings should be clearly legible from about three metres, and not be larger than is necessary. Remember headings should be informative and not obtrusive. Titles should be in simple, clear lettering for younger children, but older children will be able to appreciate more unusual letter forms that reflect the mood of the display.

For small headings fibre-tip pens and the broad-nibbed felt markers are suitable. For special displays transfer lettering, such as Letraset, might be applicable. For extra large headings letters may be cut from coloured paper. These could be traced from the large posters often seen outside newsagents, or cork display letters could be used as templates.

Materials and equipment

This list is not meant to be an exhaustive list and many of the items are standard in the majority of schools.

It includes all of the items mentioned under the Resources needed part of the Session plans, so should prove useful to any head teacher or teacher with a post of responsibility for art who wishes to order and collect materials for the school.

It is generally accepted that most primary schools are on quite a tight budget, and it is unlikely that money will be available for very sophisticated materials. For this reason, the following list may appear somewhat basic to some of our larger schools, which have managed to build up a comprehensive range of equipment over the years.

Should teachers wish to increase the range of art and craft activities, the list of suppliers should prove useful.

Paper and card

For all but a few of the Sessions, almost any sort of paper would do. It is absolutely amazing how much perfectly good paper is thrown away by various organisations, so before buying anything it is advisable to write to parents to suggest sources of their own. If this fails, then contact local paper makers, printers, newspaper offices, department stores, computer centres or anywhere that uses paper. I know of at least one very large primary school that has not *bought* paper for years, but this hasn't restricted art and craft in the school. Remember, too, that specialist paper suppliers are usually cheaper than contractors.

Newspaper This has so many uses in the school and should never be underated because it is free and plentiful. Besides being invaluable for model-making of all sorts, it is quite adequate for experiments in printing and painting. In fact, in painting it has some advantages over plain paper. Young children might be encouraged to mix their paint thickly and cover the entire paper. Also, children need not feel restricted by expense when engaged in experimental work. How many times have we heard 'Can I start again?' after a child has made a false start?

Wrapping paper This is much tougher than newspaper and is most useful as a backing to collage work and, when several pieces are stuck together, may be used as a backing for large-scale paintings and collages.

Wallpaper Shops will give away old sample books and parents will give ends of rolls. The plain side is fine for painting, collage and friezes. The patterns are useful for exercises in colour, pattern, texture, collage, covering folders or even acting as a backing for displays.

Bank paper Sometimes called typewriting paper or detail paper. It is excellent for drawing, rubbings and tracing where fine detail is not called for. It can be bought in a variety of sizes but A4 typewriting size is very useful.

Newsprint and kitchen paper These two are similar and look like newspaper without the print. Useful for drawing, painting, paste, paperwork and particularly for any printing, as it is slightly absorbent.

Brushwork paper This is like a heavy kitchen paper but comes in a variety of colours.

Sugar paper This is much heavier and tougher than brushwork paper and comes in a greater variety of colours. It is particularly useful as mounting for temporary displays only, as the colours quickly fade in the sunlight.

Cartridge paper This is good quality drawing paper, usually white or cream in colour. As it is very expensive it should only be used on special occasions for drawing, or as a substitute for card when doing paper sculpture or model making.

Tissue paper Translucent and brightly coloured, this is useful for collage work, as a final coating to paste paper models and for decorative designs hung against the light or the windows.

Silver or metallic paper Extremely expensive to buy but a useful stock of chocolate sweet covers and kitchen foil could be collected by the children.

Cardboard boxes and corrugated card These are invaluable for model-making. Cut up some of the boxes and store the card flat.

Manilla board This is an inexpensive board that comes in a variety of colours and is useful for more special or long-lasting displays, as it does not fade noticeably.

Strawboard This is a useful board for booklet covers and craftwork that requires a really rigid board. It comes in three thicknesses. The thinnest is about twice the weight of a cereal packet and the thickest is about the thickness of hardboard.

Graph paper Two sizes are useful – the 1 cm squares and the 1 cm squares broken down into even smaller squares.

Transparent self-adhesive sheeting This comes in rolls of various widths and is useful for special work that needs covering, like pressed leaf pictures, calendars, etc.

Cellophane paper A good supply of waste could be built up
for collage work. Particularly useful for work on colour theory (optical mixing
of colour) and designs on windows or projected on to large screens or walls
(Session 103).

Carbon paper Useful for tracing down designs.

Paints

Preferences amongst teachers vary tremendously. Powder colour has been the
accepted paint for many years, but recently the choice of paints has widened.
It has been the practice of manufacturers to offer teachers at least twenty
different colours which, I feel, is quite unnecessary, and has led to some
confusion.

From about eight well-chosen colours it should be possible to mix just about
any colour likely to be needed. So the problem is, which eight, and how much
of each should be ordered. The section dealing with colour on page 145 should
help you to decide which colours to choose. The question of how much of each
colour is trickier to answer, but, generally speaking, about three times as much
white should be ordered as any other colour.

Powder colour This would seem to be the most economical way of buying paint
but, in practice, tends to be messy and wasteful when used in the plastic bun
trays found in most schools. For infant classes, however, where the paint is
usually mixed in jam jars, this is fine. So, too, when large areas of colour are
needed and the paint is mixed in bowls. Surprisingly little water should be
added to the dry colours, a few drops at a time until a rich, creamy paint is
made.

Tempera blocks These are more convenient and less messy than powder
colour, if only small quantities of colour are required, but it is difficult to mix
up a thick, creamy paint to cover large areas, and brushes suffer from
continuous scrubbing.

Ready-mixed paints These come in plastic squeezy bottles, mixed to a creamy
consistency and can be squeezed straight into a palette or tray. With
experience children waste very little as dried paint may be moistened and
added to. It is essential, however, to keep the colours clean and to mix colours
in a separate tray or on a palette.

Gold and silver spray aerosols These are expensive and should be used only for
special occasions where particular decorative effects are called for (Session
79).

Materials allied to paints

Brushes This is one item where it rarely pays to buy the cheapest. Two types of brush are needed:
a) *Hog-hair or bristle.* Good quality brushes are needed for the rough jobs like scrubbing in large areas of colour or paste papering models. A variety of both flat and round in sizes 8, 10 and 12 would be suitable.
b) *Water-colour brushes.* Usually made of sable, ox or squirrel hair, or a blend. They are essential for finer work usually with the older children. One set for a school would be appropriate consisting of sizes 2, 5 and 6.

Palettes The most useful type is probably the plastic bun-tin type, which can be used for holding colour and mixing colour. It is better for children to have a separate palette for each of these jobs.

Water jars Heavy, large jars that will not tip over easily are essential. Specially designed non-spill jars are on the market, but large coffee or jam jars are quite suitable, though potentially more accident prone. Small plastic cups are hopeless for water jars. Water should be changed as soon as it gets dirty.

Paint rags Any absorbent material about the size of a handkerchief will do. Essential for keeping colours clean in the palette.

Overalls These should cover as much of the child as possible. A man's shirt cut off at the elbows and buttoned at the back takes a lot of beating.

Drawing materials

Pencils If possible, children should be given the opportunity to try the full range from 4H (very hard), 2H, H, HB, (normal), 2B, to 4B (very soft).

Charcoal If you don't feel inclined to buy this, make some by burning twigs.

Wax crayons A very versatile colouring medium, capable of a great variety of effects.

Ball-point, felt and fibre-tip pens Excellent for detailed drawing and fine pattern work. Most children have their own, but extra black ones are always needed.

Pen and ink This is usually reserved for the older children who realise that fibre-tip pens have certain limitations.

Experimental pens Children should be encouraged to make their own pens by sharpening the ends of twigs, old paint brushes, etc.

Chalk Useful for backgrounds where colours need to be merged.

Adhesives

PVA Probably the most versatile adhesive available. It is a thick, white plastic-based glue that will stick most things together. Heavy items like wood and cardboard models might need to dry for several hours, but fabric and paper needs only minutes. PVA can be diluted with water to make it go further as a paper adhesive, but is waterproof when dry and very difficult to remove from clothes and brushes. For this reason it is advisable to apply it with strips of cardboard or plastic spatulas, from which the PVA peels off when dry. Five litre containers are the most economical. The PVA is dispensed into yoghurt cartons. At the end of the day it can be poured back into the container. Diluted 50/50 with water, PVA serves as a varnish for paintings and models, or it may be mixed with powder or ready-mixed colour, to form a tough, waterproof paint suitable for strengthening models. Paint mixing should be done in disposable containers like yoghurt cups, as dried paint with PVA is very difficult to remove from palettes.

Powder paste This is mixed with water and is useful, and more economical, than PVA when a lot of glue for paperwork is needed. Added to pulped-down newspaper it makes papier mâché, a valuable modelling compound.

Impact adhesive e.g. Bostik and Evostick. This is handy where strong joins need to be made quickly. Just a smear of adhesive is applied to both surfaces, allowed to dry and then put and held together. They join immediately.

Gum e.g. Cow Gum. This is applied in the same way as impact adhesive, but is not as strong or expensive.

Latex e.g. Copydex. This is very quick drying and is especially useful on fabric, for cardboard models or for mounting as it does not cause the paper to cockle. But, beware, as it is impossible to remove from clothes unless you buy a special solvent from the makers.

Fabric dyeing (Sessions 85, 112, 113, 114.)

The most easily available and versatile range of dyes are probably made by Dylon. As with most goods, it is cheaper to buy dye in large quantities, rather than the small tins of dye found in most chemists or hardware shops. Colours can be mixed, so it is better to buy large quantities of, say, the three primary colours than a large range of colours in small quantities. Some cold water dyes, and a tin of Paintex, will serve the needs of all the Sessions in this book where cotton fabrics are mentioned. Dylon also provide excellent, free instruction leaflets. Synthetic materials, however, need special dyes. Fabricrayon transfer crayons offer exciting possibilities and go a long way. They come in a packet of eight colours, and may be purchased from general suppliers and some art shops. For small classroom projects the only other equipment necessary for fabric dyeing is rubber gloves, salt, household soda, buckets, mallet or hammer, smoothing iron and spoons.

Claywork (Sessions 21, 22, 28, 60, 119, 120.)

Clay It is best to start with ready-to-use earthenware clay that fires at a temperature of about 970°C. It is cheaper to purchase clay from a specialist firm and, obviously, the larger the order the more economical it becomes. It might pay to make enquiries of local firms that use clay, who might be willing to sell you the odd bag. Remember to keep the bag tightly sealed to avoid the clay drying out.

A dustbin Put a few housebricks at the bottom and 10 cm of water. Lay some damp sacking over the bricks. When the children have odd pieces of clay over at the end of the session, or if dry clay models are to be re-constituted they are put on the sacking and covered with another layer of sacking. In time the clay absorbs the moisture and returns to malleable clay again.

Modelling boards These can be offcuts of plywood.

Modelling tools Spatulas, lolly sticks, spoons.

Cloths Absorbent fabric for keeping the clay moist.

Rolling pins Or pieces of broom handle for rolling out the clay.

Old dustbin or five gallon oil drum To make a sawdust kiln (Session 120).

Sawdust For firing the kiln. The very fine sawdust from a sawmill or joinery is best. As it must be bone dry, it should be collected a week beforehand and placed in a warm, dry spot.

Boot and furniture polish In the absence of glazing facilities, fired models and pots can be finished off by rubbing in plenty of wax polish and shining with a soft brush.

Printing (Sessions 47, 53, 72, 73.)

Most of the printing at this level comes under the general headings of block printing or press printing. Blocks might be made from potatoes or lino and press prints can be made from just about anything fairly small that can be inked and pressed on to paper to build up a picture, or part of one, e.g. a piece of card, the end of a pencil, fingers, etc.

Inks Oil-based or water-based – the former being permanent but messy to clear up and expensive.
Water-based printing ink, on the other hand, is fairly permanent, except when put out in the rain, and equipment is washed with water. The advantages of printing ink over paint is that it is relatively slow drying, easily and quickly applied to blocks and provides an even layer of colour necessary for printing. The large tubes may appear to be expensive, but, if the ink is rolled out correctly to a thin layer, it goes a very long way. Ink is the consistency of toothpaste and colours may be mixed with a palette knife on any smooth surface. A set of primary colours and black and white, should prove sufficient.

Printing rollers As this is definitely a small group activity, four rollers should be sufficient – two of 4 cm and two of 8 cm.

Formica sheets About 20 × 30 cm for rolling out the ink.

Sharp knives for cutting blocks.

Palette knives for mixing inks. The plastic ones are unsuitable for this.

Plaster of Paris

This can be purchased at chemist's or from general suppliers of art materials. It works out much cheaper to buy a large bag, but this must be stored in dry conditions or it will go off and become unuseable.
Cover work surfaces with newspaper, estimate how much water it takes to fill your mould and pour this amount into a mixing bowl that will hold at least twice as much. The best types of bowl to use are made of flexible plastic. Sprinkle plaster of Paris into the water and stir continuously with an old stick until you reach a consistency of custard, i.e. the plaster should pour easily but not be very runny. It should settle in the mould with a flat surface. Half-fill the mould, stir the plaster in the bowl then continue filling. Any excess plaster should be poured into paper cups and used later for carving. If the consistency is correct it will start to set almost immediately, and be hard after thirty minutes. If it is still very damp after this time, not enough plaster was added and the cast will be weak.
If it starts to set as it is being poured, then too much plaster has been added.
Important. Plaster should never be poured down the sink as it will block it as it sets. Throw the mixing stick away. Let the plaster in the bowl set then crack it into a dustbin by bending the bowl.

Waste materials

In recent years teachers have become fully aware of the tremendous potential for producing exciting, creative work from materials destined for the dustbin. Many have reached the stage that hardly anything can be thrown away in case it comes in handy.

Of course, with small classrooms and large classes, storage is a constant headache, so the teacher is forced to improvise. The problem is to devise a system that will encourage the children to keep a tidy classroom and to respect materials commonly referred to as 'junk'.

One way to overcome the problem of storing a huge range of miscellaneous items is to label as many shoeboxes as you can get hold of, and to stack these on shelves, on cupboards or in a corridor. Ask children to bring in items and keep them topped up. The collection could perhaps be shared by two or more classes. The following list might be the starting point for this collection and includes most of the materials suggested in the sessions that need to be brought in at one time or another by the children or teachers.

String, wool, raffia.
Beads, buttons, stones, seeds.
Lentils, pasta.
Washing-up liquid bottles.
Cardboard tubes.
Offcuts of green fabric.
Offcuts of red fabric.
Offcuts of green paper.
Offcuts of red paper.

Polystyrene offcuts.
Thin foam rubber.
Feathers.
Plastic bags.
Cocktail sticks, matches.
Yoghurt cartons.
Corks, cotton reels.
Shiny paper, bottle tops, silver paper.

Miscellaneous items

This is simply a list of all the items mentioned in the Session outlines that do not fall neatly into any of the above categories. Everything may be bought locally or from one of the educational suppliers.

Materials Dressmaking pins; Plasticine; Selotape, elastic bands; needles and cotton; plaster of Paris; small calendars; fixative; paper doylies; table tennis balls; 35 mm slide mounts (from photographic dealer); coloured inks, drinking straws; galvanised wire 18 gauge (from hardware shops).

Equipment Scissors; slide projector; record player or tape recorder; plastic spatulas for glue; rulers; stapler and staples; plastic mixing bowls; compasses; guillotine or rotary paper cutter; spray diffusers; clipboards with bulldog clips for sketching; wire cutters; pliers; sharp knives.

Stain removal from clothes

Even water-based paints stain clothes and sometimes it is impossible to completely remove stains, especially dye stains. Prevention is better than cure and a protective apron or overall is strongly recommended for all art and craft work.

Water-based paints Let the paint dry. Brush it off then hand-wash in warm, soapy water. If this doesn't work, try dry cleaning.

Oil-based paints Treat the stain before it dries, if possible. Dab gently on both sides of the fabric with a clean cloth soaked with white spirit, then wash in warm, soapy water. The garment may still need dry cleaning.

PVA or acrylics Treat the stain before it dries if possible. Dab gently on both sides of the fabric with a clean cloth moistened with water, then wash in warm, soapy water. If the stain has already dried, pick it off as much as possible then rub with methylated spirit. The garment may still need dry cleaning.

Dyes Treat before it dries if possible. Wash with hot water and washing powder. Dylon International supply a stain remover called Dygon which removes most stains from white fabrics, but coloured fabrics must be colour fast before using it.

Suppliers

Nearly everything on the materials and equipment list may be obtained from one of the suppliers of general art and craft materials. Schools may also have a supplies department within the authority that acts as an agent for a great number of firms.

It is often worthwhile, however, to seek out specialist suppliers, who may be able to offer a wider choice cheaper than the general supplier.

Many of the suppliers listed below offer an excellent advice service to teachers with free literature on the use of their materials, and where to purchase them.

General art supplies
A. Brown,
Perth Street West,
Hull.

Berol Ltd.,
Old Meadow Road,
Kings Lynn
Norfolk. PE30 4JR.

Educational Supply Association Ltd.,
Pinnacles,
Harlow,
Essex.

Nottingham Educational Supplies,
17 Ludlow Hill Road,
West Bridgford,
Nottingham.

Reeves & Sons,
Lincoln Road,
Enfield, Middx.

George Rowney & Co., Ltd.,
10–11 Percy Street,
London W1.

Winsor & Newton Ltd.,
Wealdstone,
Harrow, Middx.

J. Bryce Smith Ltd.,
117 Hampstead Road,
London N.W.1.

Dryad,
Northgate,
Leicester.

Dyes
Dylon International Ltd.,
139 Sydenham Road, S.E. 26.

Skilbeck Bros. Ltd.,
Bagnall House,
55–57 Glengall Road,
London S.E.15.

Beads and sequins
The Bead Shop,
53 South Molton Street,
London W.1.

Ells & Farrier,
5 Prince Street,
London W.1.

Plaster of Paris
Boots the Chemist.

Embroidery
Embroiderers Guild,
36 Manchester Street,
London W.1.

Thomas Hunter,
Northumberland Street,
Newcastle on Tyne.

Mace & Nairn,
89 Crane Street,
Salisbury, Wilts.

Pottery
Mills and Hubball Ltd.,
Victoria Rise,
Clapham Common,
London S.W.4.

Podmore & Sons Ltd.,
Shelton,
Stoke-on-Trent.

Wengers Ltd.,
Stoke-on-Trent,
Staffs.

Paper and card
Allen-Glenold,
Glenold House,
East Farndon,
Market Harborough,
Leics. LE16 9SJ.

Hunt and Broadhurst Ltd.,
Botley Road,
Oxford.

Paperchase,
216 Tottenham Court Road,
London W.1.

Puppetry
Waldo S. Lanchester,
The Puppet Centre,
Stratford-upon-Avon,
Warwicks.

Printing
T. N. Lawrence & Son Ltd.,
2–4 Bleeding Heart Yard,
Greville Street,
Hatton Garden, London E.C.1.

Screen printing
Sericol Group Ltd.,
24 Parsons Green Lane,
London SW6 4H

Glossary of terms

Appliqué A pattern or design made by sticking or sewing pieces of fabric together. Session 115, 94.

Asymmetry The opposite of symmetry. A design where the two sides do not balance each other.

Batik Designs are made by forming a resist with hot wax painted or dripped on to fabric, which is then allowed to cool before being dyed.

Block printing Printing on to paper or fabric with a block cut from lino, potato, etc. Session 113.

Blutack A putty-like substance used to display pictures. Will adhere to most surfaces, but stains some porous ones.

Box puppet A puppet based on a cardboard box. Session 100.

Ceramics or pottery Clay objects that have been fired in a kiln.

Clay See page 158.

Collage Making pictures by sticking miscellaneous items to a backing sheet or board. Sessions 18, 19, 24, 27, 29.

Colour See page 145.

Complementary colours Colours that are directly opposite to one another in the colour wheel. Session 51, 102.

Composition Putting together all or some of the basic elements of art (line, colour, tone, texture, form, pattern, shape) so that there is a satisfactory relationship between them.

Counterchange Usually refers to a type of pattern making, when dark and light shapes alternate. Session 81.

Crayon etching See Session 75.

Diffuser Implement for spraying fixative or thin paint or ink.

Dustbin kiln See sawdust kiln.

Earthenware A low-fired type of pottery. See clay on page 158.

Elements of art Colour, tone, line, shape, pattern, texture, form. See page 145.

Fingerpaints A glutinous paint, usually used by infants to create patterns on smooth surfaces with their fingers. Paints may be purchased. These can be worked for a very long period of time before they start to dry; they wash off hands and clothing easily. Fingerpaints can also be made by adding any water-based paint to a thick wallpaper paste or a colourless gel, e.g. Reeve's Gelmix. Session 16.

Fixative Colourless liquid that is sprayed on to charcoal and chalk drawings to prevent smudging.

Form See page 149.

Frieze Historically it is the area between the architrave and cornice of a Greek temple. In schools this refers to an elongated strip of paper decorated in a variety of ways.

Galvanised wire Comes in various thicknesses. Gauge 18 or 20 is best for modelling purposes.

Glove puppet	A puppet that fits over the hand so that the thumb and little finger work the arms of the puppet. Session 99.
Hessian	A coarsely-woven fabric similar in texture to sacking. Comes in a variety of colours and is suitable for appliqué.
Hue	Colour at its brightest intensity.
Impact adhesive	See the section on adhesives, page 157.
Intensity	The relative greyness of a colour.
Kiln	An oven that reaches very high temperatures, turns clay to pottery.
Latex	See the section on adhesives, page 157.
Line	See page 145.
Marbling	Thin, oily paint is floated on to a tray of water. Patterns are made by gently stirring the paint and placing a sheet of paper on to it.
Medium	The material used to produce art, e.g. paint, clay, charcoal.
Mobiles	Constructions suspended from cotton or string, usually from the ceiling, which move around slowly.
Monoprinting	A shiny surface is rolled with printing ink. A design is made by scratching into the ink. Thin paper is placed on top and rubbed gently to transfer the design. Alternative in Session 73.
Mosaic	Pictures and designs are made by imbedding small pieces of tile, stones or glass into plaster or cement.
Mural	Strictly speaking, it is a painting done straight on to a wall. In schools any large painting is usually referred to as a mural.
Negative printing	See Session 72.
Neutral colours	Usually refers to white, grey and black.
Observational drawing	Drawing whilst studying an object or environment first hand.
Papier mâché	Made by soaking shredded newspaper in a bucket of water, then stirring in paste powder until the mixture reaches the consistency of dough.
Pattern	See page 147.
Plaster casting	Plaster is poured into a prepared mould of Plasticine or clay. Session 93.
Plaster of Paris	A white powder which, when mixed with water to the correct consistency, sets hard. Used mainly for casting and carving. Session 93.
Press printing	Pictures are made by pressing small objects (corks, bottle tops, etc.) on to paper after being charged with ink or paint. Session 47.
Primary colours	Colours that cannot be made from mixing other colours. Yellow, red, blue. Session 51.

Proportion	The relative size of one shape to another, or amount of one colour to another.
PVA	Poly-vinyl acetate. A plastic based adhesive. See the section on adhesives, page 157.
Paste paper	Newspaper is torn into small pieces and pasted on to models, etc. to provide extra strength. The pieces should overlap slightly.
Relief rubbing	Rubbings are made from built up surfaces of paper or card. Session 78.
Reproductions	Copies of work by famous artists. These may be purchased from major art galleries, but many local authorities have loan systems. Sessions 70, 102, 107, 108, 110, 116, 117.
Rod puppet	A puppet with a rod or stick running through it which is held by the puppeteer. Session 99.
Rubbings	Thin paper is placed on a textured surface and rubbed with a pencil or crayon. Sessions 17, 71, 78.
Sawdust kiln	Also known as a dustbin kiln. Pots are dried and loaded into a dustbin or oil drum packed with sawdust, which is set alight. Session 120.
Scale	The relative size of a drawing or painting to the actual subject being studied.
Secondary colours	A mixture of two of the primary colours. Session 51.
Shade	When black is added to a primary or secondary colour, a shade of the original colour is produced.
Shape	See page 148.
Spatula	A tool for applying or spreading adhesives.
Spray diffuser	See diffuser.
Straw blowing	Blobs of runny paint or ink are put on to a sheet of paper, then blown in all directions with a drinking straw. Session 39.
Symmetry	Exact correspondence of opposite sides of a design or object, to each other.
Template	A shape which serves as a guide for reproducing that shape, e.g. a jam jar lid might be used as a template for drawing a circle.
Texture	See page 147.
Texture rubbings	See rubbings.
Three-dimensional	Forms which have depth or are surrounded by space, as opposed to being flat.
Tie and dye	Material is bound with string or elastic bands and dipped into dye. Session 85, 112.
Tint	When white is added to a primary or secondary colour, a tint of the original colour is produced.
Tonal contrast	The effect of a dark colour next to a light colour, or a light and dark shade of the same colour.

Tone　　　　　　　　A way of referring to the lightness or darkness of colours, see page 146.

Transfer printing　Printing ink is applied to a surface and then transferred to paper. Sessions 53, 114. Fabricrayons are used to transfer a crayon drawing on to synthetic fabric.

Two-dimensional　On a flat plane.

Vegetable printing　Printing blocks are made by cutting vegetables in half, dipping into paint or dye and pressing on to paper or fabric. Vegetables used include potatoes, carrots, brussel sprouts.

Viewfinder　　　　A rectangle of paper or card with a rectangular hole cut in it. Useful for sketching to isolate a subject. Session 91.

Wax resist　　　　Watery paint is washed over a wax crayon drawing or rubbing. Session 75.

Window pictures　If washing-up liquid is added to paint, pictures may be painted directly on to windows and removed by washing. Stained glass effects may be achieved by making pictures from translucent materials, e.g. tissue, or Cellophane paper.

Bibliography

Aims into Practice in the Primary School	P. Ashton	Hodder & Stoughton
Children Solve Problems	E. de Bono	Penguin
Primary Education in England	D.E.S.	H.M.S.O.
Educating Artistic Vision	E. Eisner	Collier Macmillan
The Psychology of Children's Drawings	H. Eng	Routledge & Kegan Paul
Artful Scribbles	H. Gardner	J. Norman
Exploring Visual Design	J. Gatto	Davis Publications
Pre-School and Infant Art	K. Jameson	Studio Vista
Junior School Art	K. Jameson	Studio Vista
The Language of Vision	G. Kepes	Theobald
Creative and Mental Growth	V. Lowenfield	Collier Macmillan
Visual Awareness	S. Palmer	Batsford
The Drawing Handbook	R. Purser	Davis Publications
Sight and Insight	K. Rowland	Longman
A History of the Modern Movement	K. Rowland	Van Nostrand Reinhold
An Eye on the Environment	H. B. Joicey	Unwin Hyman

The books listed below provide more detailed information in all of the techniques mentioned in this book, and also some techniques that there has not been room for.

Art and Craft Today	H. Pluckrose	Bell & Hyman

(Batik, crayonwork, drawing, decorating, fabric collage, fabric printing, finger painting, masks, mosaics, needlework, painting, paperwork, paper sculpture, patternwork, printing, puppetry, tie and dye, wooden models.)

The Art and Craft Book	H. Pluckrose	Bell & Hyman

(Batik, fabric, printing, junk modelling, mobiles, modelling, monoprinting, painting, paperwork, paper sculpture, pattern work, pen and ink, polystyrene, printing, puppetry, reproductions, sawdust kilns, stencilling, straw blowing.)

Simple Printmaking	Kent	Studio Vista
Puppetry Today	Binyon	Studio Vista
Creative Rubbings	Andrew	Batsford
Creative Papercraft	E. Rottger	Batsford
Make it in Paper	M. Grater	Bell & Hyman
Masks	R. Slade	Faber
Embroidery in the Primary School	A. Butler	Batsford
Introducing Textile Printing	N. Proud	Batsford
Tie and Dye	A. Maile	Bell & Hyman
Pottery in the Primary School	D. Cummings	Muller
Making Mobiles	A. & C. Moorey	Studio Vista
Exploring Papier Mâché	V. Betts	Davis
You Can Draw	K. Jameson	Studio Vista

Some of these books may be out of print but still available in libraries.